The Forgotten

Lynn Robinson

The Forgotten
By Lynn Robinson

First Published 2020
Copyright © Lynn Robinson

The rights of the author have been asserted in accordance with Sections 77 and 78 of the Copyright Designs and Patents Act, 1988.

All rights reserved.

IBSN: **978-1-8380268-0-6**

DEDICATION

To my husband, our children, and grandchildren, for showing me the meaning of unconditional love. For your hugs and kisses, your craziness and for our dancing queen Sunday afternoons.
For my friends who have helped me through some hard times and shown me the true meaning of friendship.
I love you loads.

Acknowledgements

For my family and friends who have walked beside
me through thick and thin.
Showing love and support, never judging, and always
giving sound advice.

For my clients who have put their trust in me even on
their darkest days you are braver than you think and
stronger than you know.

For all of you reading this book, who have suffered
with any form of mental health, I believe in you.

A Special thank you to my friends and fellow authors,
Estelle Maher, Jeanette M Moore and Bob Stone of
Write blend bookstore in Waterloo Liverpool, for
your help in bringing this book to publication.

And finally thank you to my cover designer
Emma Sandison
For bringing my book to life.

For having you all in my life, I am truly blessed.

Forward

When enough of the children are awake, we will witness a significant change in the world. There will be freedom from fear and negativity, and we will see a higher level of consciousness which will lead to a greater understanding of heaven and the astral realms. Which will bring a better way of life for humanity.

These children have been biding their time waiting for the right moment to come and save our planet, returning harmony and ending this chaos and disorder in our world. New teachings will come to us and eventually our countries and the world will be governed by these amazing souls. They also tell us that, love and compassion, will be the forces that guide the union of the people.

There have been people, lightworkers in place for 50 years or more preparing for the arrival of these children. Mother Earth has had a significant part in placing these lightworkers around the globe. She has kept a close contact within meditations and channelings to enable us to be safe and prepare for what is to come. Most of these lightworkers have recreated themselves in some way, and this transition has not been an easy one.

This time will be welcomed by many of us lightworkers. It will bring an end to the way of life as we know it and the beginning of a new way of thinking. A new way of being will be shown to us, and we will help the world to join as one with the earth and nature once again. Just as we have been taught in our groups over the past years, we will be as the shamans.

The Great Change has already begun and brings the promise of a new human being. We need to re-learn to honor and respect Mother Earth and lightworkers. We need to discover and appreciate everything, be able to make a significant leap towards what we are becoming, and all work together.

The new age will announce the beginning of the sixth sun, that will be the time of the "children of light" who will be fully awake. The energies that these children will radiate is so powerful that you cannot help but love them.

There of course will be those who do not want these souls to shine and will do everything in their power to stop this awakening. But you cannot stop it the inevitable will happen, and light will succeed dark. Each one of you, look at your children, your grandchildren, as they already walk amongst us.

Learn from nature and mother earth she is a power that must not be reckoned with. Connect to the planet as a whole, the water, the trees, the beautiful mountains and honour Mother Earth's great spirit. But most of all honour who you are and be the best possible version of you.

The Forgotten

"Why? Why this title?" I asked my Spirit Guides.

"Well, let me tell you a story." came the answer.

I sat and listened with tears rolling down my face. This was my life they were talking about; these were my children. I questioned myself more than once as I listened to them telling me about the children of today. What was I to do? How was I able to fix the problem that we, as parents, have created for ourselves over the last few decades?

Admitting that some of the habits our children now have could partially be our fault is a hard pill to swallow. But here goes!

As a young mother, I tended to lean towards my own parents' way of bringing up my children. They sat at the table to eat their meals, they minded their manners and always said their pleases and thank you's. Over the years, as they grew from babies to young adults, I was told by many that my children were a credit to me. I was always proud to hear this, as I knew I could take my children anywhere and never worry about them having a paddy or being rude.

Recalling my own childhood, I remember that we never had the luxury of a TV in every room, never mind the bedroom. When we went to bed, we would read our book, or we would be so tired from playing out with our friends all day, that we would be asleep by the time our heads hit the pillow. There were no mobile phones then, no PC or laptops, and no gaming systems.

As I am writing this, I am recalling the controversial debates happening right now regarding 5G. I think our Government is crazy and the public is too! Everyone wants faster Internet and faster-paced lives. 5G was being developed many years ago as a weapon of destruction. 5G, 4G, 3G are all intensive wavelengths of vibrational energy, and there is no pleasant way to say this, but they are frying our brains, and our children's minds. There has been scientific proof that these waves of energy are killing off parts of the human brain and causing cancers and other illnesses. Why has there been a considerable rise in childhood illness and Childhood cancers? These are the questions that should be being asked.

Why is no one taking any notice? As I write this chapter, I am away on holiday, literally up a mountain. We are staying right in the middle of the Snowdon Range in North Wales. The mountain has a distinctive air about it; if the Earth had a pulse, it rose through these mountains, creating their bold silhouette. To my eye, their peaks are breathtakingly beautiful. Their slopes give a home to so much life and are a foundation for trees and shrubs, grass, and ferns. With blue above and below, in the sky and the lake, the energy of this place is breath-taking, and I just knew that whatever the weather, it would be a good day. Coming here is as intense as receiving incredible healing. As a family, we have been coming here for more than twenty years. Over those twenty years, nothing up here has changed, and I mean nothing! There is no Sky TV, no telephone line, and most of all, no mobile phone signal!

It is difficult to explain the freedom it gives us all. I bring my whole family to this remarkable place of sanctuary every year. There are thirteen of us; my two children and their partners, all my grandchildren, my stepson and Jess, my grandson's girlfriend. Sadly, my youngest son is not with us. He has suffered from anxiety for twenty-four years and this year, after losing his nan, my mum, it has been particularly bad. So, he could not face making the trip. This saddened me significantly, but it is a process he must go through, and so again, the work begins, on lifting my son out of the darkness in which he lives and back into the light.

My family look forward to coming here, and no one moans about not having Internet or phone signals. We sit as a family, and we talk, we play board games, we play with the little ones, we walk around the beautiful lakes, and the best is the laughter. The memories I have been building up here are priceless, but one day they will look quite primitive. I would imagine that our adventures and family times would look primaeval to many now! With many families flying all over the world in search of something adventure, I fear they are missing the point, the simple things in life are the most treasured, I feel. Don't get me wrong I love the sunshine as much as the next person, but no holiday could replace the times I have spent with my family.

This, I am sure you are thinking, sounds like a well-structured family. Yes, it is, but it is not without its trials and tribulations, believe me. The truth is that most parents do their best for their children and try to make life as beautiful as possible. Along the way, we do make bad choices. Not every decision we make is a good one because we are only human. Not all parents will admit to this, but as a parent, we too make choices that can change the way a child lives their lives.

I was born in the 1960s and came from a hard-working family. Both my parents went out to work, and we children would be looked after by Aunties and Uncles, some of whom were called that, but were not actually blood relations. In those days, the community came together and helped each other out. I have many happy memories of times spent with my Auntie Doreen and Uncle Andrew. They lived in a little bungalow over the road from us when I was only two years old and often talked about them to my children and grandchildren. These were happy times. Mum and Dad had to work, so Aunty Doreen usually stepped in to give a helping hand. Mum would come home from work tired, but there was always one thing in abundance in our house, something that was free to give - LOVE.

I always look back on my childhood and feel very blessed indeed for the love and the passion my parents put into their family. In her later years, Mum would tell me how, at times, she barely made ends meet, and how she wondered how she would put food on the table for her family. My parent's prize possession was always their caravan on the island of Anglesey, caravan holidays where a cheaper commodity in those days and my siblings and I have fond memories of our times there.

What I did not realise was that through my younger years, I was learning about life by living it with my parents. How we conduct ourselves in our lives affects how our children will look at what they are doing with their own children. It is funny, isn't it, but how we behave ourselves around our children makes little clones of us. For some parents out there, that is quite a scary thought!

I think society needs to ask itself why we have a generation of kids who are out on the street stabbing and shooting each other? What went wrong? The trouble today is that no one wants to take responsibility for anything. If people could look within themselves, then perhaps the world would be a better place.

Every child is born innocent, without a wrong thought in their mind, or any stress or worry. Their innocence can be seen in their eyes and straight away each child is born with a pure heart and a contented soul. Then - *boom*! They are thrown into the real world. So there comes the question of how do some children grow up the way they do? Why do some become child offenders, rapists, murderers?

Then you have the other end of the scale, the high achievers, the children who will grow to make history, become doctors, nurses. The list is endless, but the answer is also unlimited. I do believe that the Devil is real; he is not some horned man who sits in wait around the corner. He is dark energy who lurks and watches, watches for that chink in the armour of the man, woman or child.

The same child is also subjected to the bright light of God, and in human life, there is a matter of choice. So, I would like to think most choose the light, but, unfortunately, some will prefer the darkness. It is proof that some children, no matter how they are brought up, will turn in the wrong direction. Some of these children can come from loving caring homes, but somewhere along the way, their mind turned dark, and they just lost their way. This is not a matter of status because the darkness can enter through the door of both rich and poor. It is a matter of acceptance; you either let in the light or the dark, you fight one to become the other.

Now, most parents will walk the path of the straight and narrow. Never doing harm to others, always holding out a helping hand if needed, and trying to be a good role model to those around them. This sounds like a perfect upbringing but then reality hits, your children start school, and they are thrown into the real world, the unprotected world. At home, you would make life as balanced as possible. Still, once they begin to mix with other children, you start to realise that your values are not always the same as those of other parents. This can be quite disturbing, as you have protected your child with all your might. You have given the values and life lessons, which have nurtured them, and then it feels that you have thrown them to the lions.

As a society, we must send our children to school, or we will be prosecuted, so we follow like sheep and do as we are told. Some children will fly through school, quite the academic. Some will be middle of the road, and some will struggle with everything they are faced within the curriculum and begin to fear school. This is usually the first sign of any anxiety or panic within a child.

I personally have a mixture in my three children, and I have asked myself why this is many times. If all my children were brought up with the same values and the same hope in their hearts, why are they all different? Still, now I look back, I can see that they are not so different. They handled life in quite different ways, but their core worries and anxieties are the same.

My children played out in the street with their friends, and my eldest son would take himself to the park with a group of boys to play football. Each of my children was told the same things as they left the house - do not talk to strangers, look both ways when you cross the road, all stay together and be home for tea.

I had no mobile phone to check on them, and at times I didn't even have a landline phone at my house. I trusted that they had listened to what I had said and would take notice. Of course, I worried; that is what mums do. But they had to live and learn, they had to grow up, and I would hear these messages echoed around the streets by other mothers and fathers. They would come home full of dirt and starving hungry, ready for a bath and tea.

Then came the PlayStations, the X-Boxes, the first computers in the home, the mobile phones!

These are the weapons of mass destruction! Mental health is under strain since the option to stay at home has become a reality. The funny thing is that both of my sons tell me I am the one who is nuts, that these things do no harm. Mmmm, well, we will see!

We are all born with a certain amount of anxiety in our bodies. If this were not present, we would plough through life without thinking about dangers. However, we can keep stress on a leash, so to speak. There are certain times in our lives when our anxiety levels are higher than at others, and this is usually when we are under duress. But we manage to brush ourselves down and carry on.

There are also triggers to bad cases of anxiety, some of which I have watched with my own children. My eldest, Nicola, was always a quiet child, and sometimes I wondered just what was going on in that head of hers. She was carefree, and, I would say, quite a balanced child, until two critical things happened simultaneously in her young life. She adored two men in her life at that time, and both were taken in an instant from her at the age of seven. My father died after a two-year battle with lymphoma, and Nicola's father left the family home and walked out on us in the same week! After that, her father only popped back into her life when it suited him. Nicola was angry about both these losses and rebelled against the one who stayed. That person, of course, was me.

This was heart breaking for me, but as her mother, I continued to plough through life doing my best. It wasn't until later in her life she would recognise that what had happened in her young life had a ripple effect on her adult life. As a teenager, Nicki's life went off the rails for a good while, and I felt I had lost control of the situation and was powerless to change anything. There were times when I wanted to lock her away from society and keep her safe, but of course, I could not. As a parent, you can protect and nurture your children, but once they are young adults, they make their own choices, and some of them can lead to tears, that is for sure. Those tears usually belong to the parents.

These times brought great strain on us as mother and daughter, but one thing I learnt from my parents, especially our Mum, was that you never give up on your own child; you keep on going until they hear your voice calling them back. That was great advice, as there were many times, I thought I had lost Nicola, but she came home, just as Mum said, and our relationship is now stronger than ever. She has the family values instilled into her that you do not ever give up on one of your children, no matter how painful it may feel at times. You are their rock; you are home to them.

Nicki now has three children of her own. She has been epileptic since she was a tiny child and fights a constant battle with her illness. Because of her epilepsy, she suffers some social anxiety and can struggle with life. She does not suffer fools lightly and does, at times, shut herself away from society. But she is a good mum and tries her best to bring her children up well. Her journey has been burdened with some bad choices, but as my Guides have told me, these are choices that every human must face. They must learn to live with the decisions that they have made, and if they are wrong ones, it is up to them to correct them and make things right.

David

My eldest son, David, was the model baby. He was so loving and showed it all the time, he was as cute as a button. He had white-blonde hair and beautiful blue eyes. Unlike his big sister, he would sleep very well from the moment he was born, and he would wake in the morning with a smile that would melt an iceberg. This little boy melted my heart; he was always cheerful but quiet around those who he did not know so well.

David was such a good boy and had hugs and kisses for everyone. Unlike his sister, he started nursery so that I could work, as their father had left us when David was only three years old. David loved nursery, and I mean he loved it. This beautiful boy had hugs and smiles for all the nursery assistants, and they told me that he interacted well. But like his big sister, he had trouble with his speech and began speech therapy at the age of four. David had his big sister wrapped around his little finger; she only had to look at him, and she would tell me what it was he wanted.

As this book unfolds, you realise that this is a form of telepathy and we are born with this skill, but because we are raised by adults, adults who have forgotten their own soul's capabilities, we are never encouraged with this ability. I bet as you are reading this, you are taking your own minds back to one of your children or grandchildren and realising that they were or are the same.

David, of course, had suffered the same losses as his sister when he was a young child. He was only three years old when his grandfather died, and his father left us. Although in our house, and to protect my children, no adult was ever allowed to talk about their father in a negative way, David still grew to hate him. The pain his Dad had caused by his neglect was unbearable. I know that this happens in a lot of family homes and children grow up well, but are they really all right? Or are they just hiding it well?

David flew through school until the age of twelve, which is when he started secondary school or 'big school' as my grandkids now call it. It was at the age of twelve that David changed. He had met up with some terrific kids, and they were reliable friends, but somehow, he seemed to find this temper from somewhere. His anger stemmed from the rejection by his father, and there was nothing I could do to fix that wound. I used to worry about him, thinking that he would get into terrible trouble with that temper of his.

I think that at times David, and I clashed, because I also had a short fuse during those times of my life. I was alone bringing up two children and it was no easy task. My ex-husband had little to offer us as a family; he was just not interested. So, I had to be the good, the bad, and the ugly and believe me it was not an easy job, but I look back now and thank God I survived. David loved his football, he lived in that park playing footy with his friends and only ever came home when he was hungry. Thankfully that anger David held is no longer with him he now seems content with his all and is a wonderful man.

David had such a love of life, and I could see it in his eyes; he was the free spirit, and he loved it. By now, I had met Ken, my youngest son's father, and my youngest son had been born. David and Ken clashed. I think it was a mixture of too much testosterone flying around in one household, but also David's anger with his own father that made him keep his distance from the only man, Ken, who was offering them a good life. Although a good man, Ken never understood David or Nicola. They were quite unruly at times, and he did not cope with that at all. I used to feel I had to be the referee to them all. It wasn't until many years later, after Ken's death, that I realised that he had issues of his own stemming from his upbringing, and so the web of darkness continued.

As David grew into an adult, he had a couple of bad relationships that well and truly crashed and burned. Then he started a job as a chef in a large local restaurant, and although it involved backbreaking work and long hours, he loved this job and I was enormously proud of him. It was then that he met his new partner. They fell in love and set up home together. I believe Ellie was sent from Heaven to help my son through what was coming, through the next part of his life, which was not going to be easy.

It was during his time as a chef that David had an accident in work. New freezers had been installed in the kitchens, and something had been spilt on the floor of the walk-in fridge. To cut a long story short, David slipped and severely damaged his ankle by ripping his ligaments and tearing his tendons. David went through surgery to try and repair his leg. Luckily there had been a witness to this happening who spoke up for David in the beginning. So, the restaurant had to pay him his sick pay, as at this time David and Ellie had a new daughter, so the worries about paying the bills were also causing stress.

It was not until a year down the line that David lost his faith in humanity. The owners of this big chain of restaurants were not interested in what had happened to him; no, they just wanted to get rid of him. So, we had to pursue it through Court. It was then we found out that the man who stood as a witness had changed his statement and told the restaurant that he didn't see anything. Strangely enough, he was promoted, to, yes, you guessed! Chef! And so, the letter came to tell David his employment was terminated. This was devastating to him as he trusted that all would go well in the end. However, there is such a thing as karma, believe me. It is not something we can send to someone; it is something that they bring to themselves. We only heard a short while ago that this man has now lost his job, so a balance has been restored.

The moral of this story is that although David was a happy-go-lucky child and young adult, circumstances in life can change things dramatically. At the young age of 33, David is struggling with what has happened to him. He permanently wears an ankle brace and is pumped up on painkillers just to get through the day. He is suffering from social anxiety since he lost his job, and I believe this is due to his self-belief and what others have done to him. He is quite an isolated man at times because of what he has been through, and we know some have been through worse, but the rejection by his father at the age of three, and a friend's lies threw David immensely. To put the cherry on the cake, we have recently bumped into the children's uncle on their dad's side, who has told us that there is a hereditary disease called Charcot-Marie-tooth disease. The whole of the family tree right down to David and Nicola's generation has been diagnosed with this illness. This is something we are now dealing with as a family, me and my two children, and their father, who lives less than two miles away, is still as aloof as ever.

There is an abundance of love in my son, and he is indeed a good man. He cares deeply about his family, and I can see it in his children's eyes how they love their daddy and that he is a good father. I am so immensely proud of him; he never fails to tell me, every time I see him or speak with him on the phone, how much he loves me. I hope and pray that one day David will find peace in his life and that the Universe will come back into alignment for him.

Christopher

Those of you who have read my other books will already know my youngest son's story. Chris is a troubled soul and is, without a doubt, one of the Crystal Children. If you haven't heard of these children before, then you will enjoy the next chapter.

Chris has struggled with anxiety his whole life from the minute he was born. I have heard every medical opinion, some of which were, "He is just a naughty child. There is nothing wrong with him that some disciplining wouldn't cure." Those comments left me both angry and sad, and I felt so alone as a mum.

He was very gentle and loving but very troubled. He really did not like anyone outside of his own safe circle. The school was a significant problem, and those sixteen years were Hell on Earth! He tried so awfully hard to fit in and, in his mind, he wanted to be a fighter pilot. He loved the aircraft which we would see at RAF Valley on Anglesey, where we would holiday many times during his young life.

One of Christopher's skills in life is that he can read people, and very well. He can pick up bad energy in the room in an instant. His skills in life outweigh my abilities as a medium, that is for sure. There are times I would have people around, and he would not come into the room; he would tell me who it was and why he didn't like them. "They will do you wrong, Mum," he would say. I would think him over-sensitive, - until they lived up to his expectations, and then I began to listen.

Chris is an intelligent young man with his whole life ahead of him, but his anxiety has imprisoned him once again. Chris does not cope with grief very well, and the loss of his father nine years ago was the first trauma to put Chris in the prison in which he lived for four years, never seeing others except those within his close family circle. We fought this battle and, with the help of Reiki healing, it released him, but for only a short while. It lasted until the death of his grandmother, my mum, who died twelve months ago, and Chris has retreated into his shell and his man-made prison, and so it begins, my fight again as a mother to release him back into the real world.

All my children were brought up the same with the same speeches from Mum as they left the house. "Don't talk to strangers, watch what you're doing when you cross the road, be home for whatever time I have given you, or there will be trouble."

None of these statements were unusual. I had said them to all my children. However, it was only in the past six years that Chris, who is now twenty-six, has told me that what I said to him worried him in his overly sensitive mind. He had taken my words literally, and really thought he would be taken by a bad person or run over on the road. As I said those things to Chris, it worried his little mind, until he could not cope. This sounds ridiculous, doesn't it? Well, as this book unfolds, you will come to realise that all children are exceptional, and every child has a special gift within their perfect little heart.

But think about this for one moment. Every child comes into the world the same, a highly evolved being with capabilities beyond belief. They can use telepathy, they can see their Spirit Guides, and they are still connected to the God source energy, the Angels and our loved ones who have gone before us.

Society, electronics, mobile phones, 5G, 4G, 3G, etc., block all these beautiful gifts in our children. This may sound far-fetched, but it is correct. We as a world are killing the minds of highly evolved children, and as we see an increase in autism, Asperger's, anxiety in many forms, we must come to realise that power and greed will be the downfall of humanity as we know it.

Are these the words of a crazy woman? NO! These are the words of the Guides and teachers of the spirit world. There is too much going on right now, and the world is dying slowly. The people of the world are up in arms over the abundance of plastic that is now killing off sea life and strangling our waterways. However, we have been told by the teachers and Guides of the spirit world that plastic is the least of our problems. The water is polluted with nuclear waste and other poisons; our sea has been dying for many years, but the tanks of waste have gone unnoticed at the bottoms of the deep oceans. Our balance on the planet is compromised, and there is little we can do to remove that mess which lies at the bottom of our oceans, but we must stop now.

The children are our future, and we have given them a hell of a clear-up job to do if humans are to survive. I have heard speeches from young children who are commenting on what we adults are doing to our planet. I would ask these children to stop and think about what they are saying. In my mum's era, going back some eighty-four years, there were no huge shopping centres and no superstores. There were corner shops and milkmen who delivered the milk in glass bottles, and those bottles were recycled every day. The corner shops used paper bags to put your vegetables in. Who are the ones who are ruining the world's balance? Is it the previous generation or is it the children who live now? This is a powerful question, but one today's children need to ask themselves! Their demands for the latest phone, faster Internet, more games consoles, lifts to school, better TV are all things I would have found alien as a child, but who had the better life? Them or me?

Coping with Anxiety

Anxiety is something everyone experiences at times. If you look at it as a built-in warning system, then it is a little easier to understand. Feeling anxious is a natural reaction to situations that we come across in our lives, but it is how we deal with those situations that determine the outcome. But sometimes feelings of anxiety can be constant, overwhelming, or out of proportion to the situation and this can affect your daily life. The good news is there are plenty of things you can try, to help you cope with anxiety.

Anxiety is a feeling of nervousness, like worry or fear that can be minor or acute. Each of us has that feeling of anxiousness from time to time, and it usually passes once the situation is over. However, in some extreme cases, the anxiety will take hold of you and cause other more frightening symptoms. Our hearts can race and give us palpitations, we can feel sweaty, shaky, and short of breath.

Anxiety can also cause changes in our behaviour. It can make us over-sensitive and make us assess everything before we do it. This, of course, is to avoid things that will trigger anxiety. I have seen this happen so many times, where avoiding anything that seems to trigger anxiety becomes the norm; therefore, you miss out on many things in your life that others are building as memories.

When stress becomes a problem, our worries can be out of proportion with relatively harmless situations. It can feel more intense or overwhelming and interfere with our everyday lives and relationships.

I hope that the stories and real life experiences in this book give you hope and reassurance that there is help out there, but the first step to receiving this help is for you to accept that you are not alone. There are many who can help you manage feelings of anxiety. But if your anxiety is affecting your daily life or causing you distress, you could consider seeking further support.

In my experience, many who struggle with mental illness first need to come to terms with what is happening to them. Document your feelings and the sensations that are making your anxiety worse. During an anxiety attack, the worst thing that my clients have told me is that they have no control over what is happening. This is where the fear comes in, that dread that stops you dead in your tracks and makes you go into your shell.

I want to help you to take back your life, take control of the emotions that are hindering you from moving on and living, instead of merely existing. So, step one is for you to take the lead and understand your anxiety. Always keep a small book with you, write in that book daily, how you feel, what symptoms you are having, and how this has stopped you from doing things that day. Do not go back too far, just work on a day-to-day basis; otherwise, it will all become very daunting and may make your mood low. If you have had a good day, don't leave that journal empty, write in it WHAT A GREAT DAY! Your mind will recognise that not every day is a bad one, which is important because when reading your own words back, you will come to realise that there are times when you do have amazing days in your life and not every day is the same.

Learn techniques that will shift your focus from bad to good. Many people find relaxation, mindfulness or breathing exercises useful. They reduce stress and focus our awareness on the present moment. By taking controlled breaths, you can slow down the symptoms of anxiety, and take back control of your own body and mind. It all sounds quite simple, but sometimes straightforward is the best. Overanalysing the situation will just bring you more stress and anxiety, so then it becomes a painful pattern. What we want to do is nip that pattern in the bud, stop it dead in its tracks and say a resounding NO!

It is easy to avoid situations or rely on habits that make us feel safer, but these can keep the anxiety going. By slowly building up time doing some things that have made you feel uncomfortable, anxious feelings will gradually reduce, and you will see these situations are not as bad as you thought.

I have been asked many times what causes anxiety, why do some have it and others not?

Anxiety affects everyone differently and can be brought on by different situations or experiences. It is our body's natural reaction to detect danger, focusing our attention and giving us a rush of adrenaline to react, sometimes called the "fight or flight" response. If you look at many different species of animal, they all have a heightened "fight or flight" mode. Sometimes it can be challenging to know what is making you anxious, which can be upsetting or stressful. That is why learning to recognise the symptoms can help, so you can deal with the insecurity better. Some people naturally react more than others, and there are times when everyone may go through stressful situations and feel anxious because of uncertainty or perceived threat.

There are lots of things that can influence our mental health, such as our upbringing, childhood environment, things that happen to us and even our temperament. There is a lot of support there to help you to cope with whatever your trigger is.

In the chapters of this book, you will see examples of this within my own children and grandchildren. Each one of my children has been brought up the same, but my manner of upbringing affected each of them differently. As a mum, this has been challenging, but I have never heard a parent say that it was the most straightforward job they ever had.

Some may experience feeling low, and again this is a part of all our lives at some time. Everyone feels upset, sad or disheartened from time to time, but for some of us, it can be a real problem. The good news is that there are things you can do to improve your mood.

Exercise is always an excellent pick up if your mood is low or you feel depressed. Going for a walk in nature releases a feel-good hormone in your body. Walking by the sea seems to energise you and blows the cobwebs away. Many things will help to lift your mood; going to a gym seems to raise a lot of people. Because again, the endorphins that are released during exercise help to lighten your mind.

Cut out that food that gives you a ten-minute high, then make you plummet back to where you started. Sugary foods are the worst for this because sugar is a quick fix, but it only gives you energy for a short time. Alcohol is another; it may give you that feeling of calm with the first glass, but once those effects wear off, you are left feeling the same.

There are many organisations that will help you to find this calm and help you to retrain your mind into finding other ways through your tough times.

As you will read, I am a spiritual medium and a double Reiki Master, holding both Usui Reiki and Karuna Reiki qualifications. Through Reiki, I have helped many whose stories you will read. Reiki brings peace and balance to your mind. If you cannot get to me, then find someone who is a qualified Reiki Master and make your first appointment. I don't think you will be disappointed. Take that first step and reach and out to someone who is willing to listen to you and encourage you with every step on your journey.

The Children of the Light

Before I explain about the children who have been brought to me for healings over the years, I want to explain to you something that was channelled to me many years ago. I must admit that I thought my imagination was running wild with me - that is until today!

Over the years, I started to have a more significant understanding of the children known as the Children of the Light, and sometimes known as the Crystal Children. Let me explain; of course, the title The Children of the Light is just a name that these kids have been given over the years. All children are unique, but you will see characteristics in the Children of the Light that make them stand out in our world, and sometimes not in a good way.

We are all born of energy, and these special children have been born on a particular energy link. Over the past eighty years or so, the link has been severely dented and the energy field in which we live has been compromised somewhat by the darker energies of war and destruction. The universal energy source, God, began to send scouts, and it was around the early 1950s, that these scouts started to awaken the planet ready for the new coming of The Children of the Light, who would begin to appear on the earth from about 1960 to present day. There are many accounts of dates and times, but I am going on what I have been told from my Guides and teachers of the spirit world.

The purpose of these Children is to bring us all into the next level in our evolution by helping to reveal in us our inner and higher selves. Without realising it, these children function as a group consciousness rather than individuals. They know why they are here and carry this knowing within their higher state, rather than in their human state. This may all sound a little bit hocus pocus but bear with me, and you will begin to see these characteristics in someone you know.

The Children are here to conquer bad, the darkness, hate and fear, and to spread love and peace, and to honour the Earth in which we live.

The Children are mostly born on what our teachers would call the Gold Ray, and this means that they have access to their natural gifts of clairvoyance and healing. They are born to the ninth dimensional level of full Christ consciousness, and their abilities are ones never seen on Earth before. They have been taught by Jesus Christ and our higher teachers to bring an absolute purity to Earth.

These children will have gained much knowledge before they came to this Earth. I hear your brain ticking over as you are reading this. No, they are not alien or extra-terrestrial beings, they are humans, but they are highly evolved humans. In the eyes of God, some of us have been here before, and we also remember our teachings from before we were born.

During channelling's, the Higher Masters and the Angels told me that I had received teachings before I came here to this life, and I was told of my life's purpose. I was prepared to receive these children, and I was informed that they would be brought to me, and others like me, one by one. These children would be all ages and they would be the ones who were suffering in many ways. The reason they are suffering is that they are different, they do not fit into the mould that society has squeezed them into. These children are highly intelligent and extremely sensitive.

I would be given a chance to help these children in a world that has labelled them. I knew that they would be struggling to understand why they feel this way, and sometimes they are pushed to the edge and cannot cope any longer.

One of the first characteristics you will notice in a Child of the light is how forgiving they are. These children are sensitive, loving and warm towards others, especially when the other person is suffering or feeling low. One of the problems with this is they are excellent empaths and can absorb the sadness that is hurting someone else, although this will be to their own downfall at times as you will see. You will notice that these children find a place to retreat, to recharge from all the negative energy.

The one thing that you must not do is see this as any sign of weakness, these Children are also compelling, and when they put their minds to something, they can move situations to their clear way of thinking in an instant.

These Children are unbelievably sensitive. They will pick up on most situations as soon as they walk into a room and because of this, you will not be able to hide anything from them. They know when you are feeling down or sad or even angry. They can also tell when someone lies to them in an instant, they will pick up body language and eye movement, and they will let this be known. They are mind readers; they know precisely what you are thinking and what is in your heart, which is another reason why they are so sensitive.

These children can reflect things back to the Universe that they feel they do not need. Not only will they reflect this energy back, but they will also send it back with more power than it was received. This may show as impoliteness in your child as they seem to go blank when they cannot absorb what you are saying or doing, and so they seem to go into a state of trance. This is a little bit of self-preservation, as they cannot absorb some of the older generation's thoughts. I have seen this so many times in my grandchildren, mostly when they are in a room full of adults. You will glance over, and they will be staring into space, completely blank. As I said, it is self-preservation.

If after reading the above, you realise that you are the parent of a Child of the light, it is always essential that your child takes in good energy or as much as possible. Be aware what surrounds your child and remove them from anything you may feel will drain them. As a parent, it is your role to help these beautiful children to reflect love, peace and oneness into the Universe and their lives.

These children do not respond to fear. We should embrace this amongst these special children, as fear seems to be magnified at this moment in time, with war and terrorism all around us on the TV and in the newspapers. Our children pick up these emotions from us. They may seem to be fearful as they lock themselves away, because, from what we can see, they cannot cope with the world. But if you speak to them about the atrocities going on in the world and to our planet, they will explain to you in detail about the whys and the wherefores of these situations.

They are listening and taking everything in. It is essential now to let go of these fears, as everything is as it should be and there is nothing to fear in this life. Even death is nothing at all; it is the end of one part of our existence and the beginning of another. Do not hide death from your children. Let them know it is okay to miss someone, but that they will see them again in another existence in the future as our energy lives on in what we believe is Heaven.

My own children have not dealt with death very well as they feel a significant loss in their hearts. I try my best to let them know that our loved ones are not gone and that we will see them again.

These gifted children will feel fear and magnify it back. If you have lower vibrational energy, you may react strongly to these children with such a high vibrational frequency. But you must remember that the energy in the Universe is changing for the better. As our vibrational frequencies are raised, a collective consciousness of peace and love is imminently returning into the world.

Please remember that some of the Children were born in the early 60s, and this means that you are now dealing with some adults who have been suffering the world's energy losses for many years. These adults may now be suffering from anxiety, panic attacks, depression, and so on. I believe that I am one of the souls who have been placed here by God to help these people, but I cannot do this alone, and so I have begun to teach what I know to others.

Over the past four years, I have held development groups, and many have joined me in trying to bring the light back to our Universe. I have been told that these people will help me to rescue the children and show them the way home. Some come and go in these groups but not many, and some, in very mysterious ways, have sometimes been removed from the groups. I would be a fool to think this was human doing. No, if they have gone, they have gone because Jesus and his teachers moved them away. None of us can do this alone; we need the security of a group so that the teachers can channel through us collectively.

We continue to work to bring love back into the world, and I believe that by writing my books it can spread the word further afield, and so awaken many light bodies who are out there feeling lost and send them the message, *You are not alone*.

Within my groups and spiritual development circles, I teach ascension; I help to clear and prepare these beautiful souls, prepare them for the higher energies that are now with us and are beginning to penetrate the Earth as I write this book. I know that we are the Circle of Elders who have been sent to heal, to make safe and to embrace the Children of the light and their work. My children and my grandchildren are a huge part of this energy growth, as I will explain later in this book. I now have a loyal circle of friends whom I know are a part of this energy and are here to help and guide as a part of their own journey.

I believe that we are a part of the scouts who arrived decades ago and came to test the waters for future Star Children. These scouts had much grief, sadness and sometimes hardships in their lives. It has taken us as a society a long time to start identifying these people and accepting them. We are all becoming crystal-like bodies, whether we realise it or not. The energy shift that is happening is supporting this energy pattern and moving us all in that direction. I know my groups will agree with this statement, as we work with these exact energies every week and can feel an immense change happening all around us. The teachers have channelled through some of my more advanced pupils and are telling them that we will work stronger as a circle, a circle of strength and trust.

This circle has not been without egos, which makes me incredibly sad. As these Children, we are put here to work collectively, not as individuals. But I know some will not be in the right place for that now; they will learn the lessons alone, but that is their choice, not mine. I can only do what I am guided to do. I trust my teachers and Guides, and I believe I will never be ready to walk this pathway alone. I am one piece in the jigsaw, and I am here to be a collective part of evolution, not a lone wolf. To walk away from such influential teachers and mentors would be suicide, but each has their own human mind, and they will do what they will do, and they will either evolve or repeat. That is all there is to the matter, as harsh as it may sound.

This energy shift is causing havoc in the world, and with each New Moon of 2019, I feel the energies becoming stronger and stronger. The many natural disasters that are occurring will continue to happen in the years to come as a result of the energy shift. It is important to remember during this time that we all must do our best to keep our souls as good and kind as possible. Always help others in need, be honest and understanding, and remember your good karma will come back to you. But so will your bad! There are many things coming that we as humans will struggle to understand. But know that the spiritual shifts are for the good of mankind and not the other way around, and whatever 2020 brings, you are supported even when you feel lost.

There is another group of highly evolved children who have started to filter into this world, and they also have been given a name by many authors. They are known as the Rainbow Children and these children are working alongside the Children of the light. They will become the new Heads of State and influential people who will begin to run our planet. The Rainbow Children have many of the same characteristics as the Crystals but are not as fearful; they have a strong will, and I believe nothing will stand in their way.

Most of these children remember their life before Earth. They come here with the ability to heal and to help others straight away. They have the most beautiful eyes and it is as if you can see straight through to their soul. They are highly intelligent, caring and extremely loving, and you will find that they have been born into a family where one or both of their parents or grandparents are either psychic or work as a medium. This mentor will help them to keep hold of their teachings and encourage them to stay a part of the heavens and the spirit world.

It seems to me as if these children have quite a task on their hands, but in time, they will help us achieve our goals and understand the perception of oneness. Fear and greed are becoming feelings of the past and will be exchanged for peace, harmony, and this sense of unity. I have come to realise that I am surrounded by these children and have noticed many of the characteristics in my children and more so in my grandchildren.

I have listed some signs that you may recognise.

- They have large eyes and an intense stare
- They are highly affectionate.
- They begin speaking later in life, but often use telepathy or self-invented words or sign language to communicate
- They are extremely connected to animals and nature
- They are usually extremely interested in rocks, crystals, and stones
- They love music and may even sing before talking
- They are extremely artistic
- They are highly empathic and sensitive

- They are forgiving and generous to others
- They draw people and animals near them and are adored by both
- They often have a good sense of balance and are fearless when exploring high places
- They often see or hear angels and Spirit Guides
- They dislike high-stress environments with many distractions
- They dislike loud/sharp sounds, such as the vacuum cleaner or electric hand dryers
- They dislike bright, unnatural lights
- They often enjoy choosing their meals
- They often speak about love and healing
- They sometimes show healing gifts at young ages
- They do not react well to sugar, caffeine, or unnatural foods/chemicals
- They dislike fighting or refuse to keep an argument going very long
- They often amplify emotional energies they gain from their environment (such as negative energies), and this can be shown in their moods
- They can become uncomfortable when around electrical devices for too long (watching TV, computer, etc.), sometimes resulting in a trance-like state
- They sometimes seem clingy to their parents until the age of four or five

- They often stare at people for extended periods (this allows them to read a person and find out more about them through their memories and energy)
- They can sometimes be controlling and show bad temper if they cannot create a reality that is good for them
- They are easily over-stimulated and need to meditate/be alone often to replenish themselves
- They may appear to be looking at nothing or talking to no one (a sign of clairvoyance and clairaudience)

It has been noticed that with many, but not all the Children, that they have delayed speech patterns. It is not surprising that delayed speech is rising in incredibly psychic children. When you think about it, why do they need to talk when they can communicate with their minds?

It is not unusual to see Crystal Children that do not speak until they're three or four years of age. It is funny watching the parent or an older sibling of a Crystal Child as they frequently become their voice because they understand entirely what it is that the child wants. I have seen all these characteristics in a few of my children and grandchildren.

The sad thing is that the medical profession often labels these very gifted but different children as having ADD or ADHD, or autism. They will say that they fit in a specific box because of their delayed speech patterns and their behaviour.

Parents should remember to look at the big picture. If their child has no trouble communicating at home, then usually they will come on fine eventually. I know this has caused distress in more than one household in my family. I can point out more than one of my family, great-nieces, great-nephews, and my own granddaughter included, where the schools have made a big fuss over the children not speaking. Then suddenly, their speech starts like an explosion, and you cannot keep them quiet.

Don't be too distressed when you know in your heart that your child communicates simply fine at home. Obviously, if your child is not talking well at home then, of course, there is a problem; most children are in their comfort zone around those who know them well. But if for any reason you feel that your child is having issues then go straight to someone who can help you.

My granddaughter Brogan is a typical Crystal Child, with 99% of the characteristics. She would sit at the back of the class and do her best not to join in. She would not answer a question, blush, and put her tongue in her cheek. The school called my daughter in many times and said her speech was not developing. On the one hand, we were grateful that they had noticed this difference in her; however, we decided we would make a video of her at home. We recorded my granddaughter chatting away, expressing all sorts of emotions on this recording, and reading the story she had written herself, at the age of four, to the camera. The teachers were shocked at what they saw and realised that my granddaughter had amazing speech and was able to pronounce some big words for her age.

My other granddaughter Ella, who is the same age, is the complete opposite, and I believe she is a Rainbow Child, as is her younger sister Holly. She has chatted since she was tiny and has also been able to heal others by touch since she was only a toddler. She is highly intelligent, and school is a breeze to her. You see, just in one family, there is a mixture of Crystals and Rainbows, who are exceptional Star Children and I am immensely proud of them.

The new generation of children of the 21st century cannot be labelled and stuck into a box. Most people are still working on the old energy vibration, so that they will find this new generation of children a bit of a challenge. It can be difficult to try and keep up with the energies that come from these new souls, but you must remember that they are coming here to help us. Some of their characteristics will seem different, and their senses escalated, but rest assured that they are not strange; they are beautiful, loving, caring individuals. I must stress that these gifts are not an excuse for bad behaviour, and we must still nurture these beautiful souls and show them strength and sound qualities, which we believe, as parents, will help them along their life's pathway.

There are many toxins and poisons in the air, and even in the unnatural way we produce food in this century. Some farmers want their stock fattened in a hurry in order to make more money. Some meat is injected with hormones to drive along the growing process, where many years ago the animals were just put in a field with long, lush grass to encourage them to put on weight. Pesticides are sprayed on vegetables, and of course, we do absorb a certain amount into our bodies.

How do we prevent this?

Apart from growing everything yourself, which is not practical any more in this fast-paced world, you can help yourself and your children in some of the following ways.

- Find a farmer who rears his own livestock and sells it through his own shop. Fresh meat is an essential form of protein

- Go to local growers for your vegetables and ask what has been used on these vegetables as pesticides

- Cook fresh food instead of tinned or pre-cooked ready meals from supermarkets

- Try and go back to basics, believe me, you will taste the difference

41

- Find a mountain retreat as I have for the past twenty years where there is no man-made interference and no distractions, somewhere your child can breathe fresh air, have a mind that is free of harmful vibrations, and live for even a short while the way we are meant to live.

The food and pesticides that we are all ingesting are shutting down our natural DNA. In the past hundred years, which in the scale of things is not a long time, we have been losing our DNA. We are now working on less than five strands of DNA, and we should be using over twenty!! This is all because of our lifestyles, what we eat, the energies around us, what is put in our drinking water etc.

We are being fed all this man-made rubbish, and the truth of it is that it is shutting us down. Look at the facts and figures. People lived healthier lives a hundred years ago. Yes, we live longer now, but we have more illnesses and disease. The reason we live longer is because the pharmaceutical companies make more medicine for us to take to combat the disease that our lifestyle is causing! Our governments make a lot of money from these industries, but is it at our expense? That is a question we all need to ask ourselves. I am not a medical person; I am a channel and this knowledge comes from a higher form of intelligence than most of us could hope to be.

Of course, we cannot control what the rest of the world is doing; however, we can make sure we look after our children and our families and take control of our destiny and theirs. Start looking into holistic treatments, because they are many centuries old and have been proven to work. Of course, there are some instances where we do need western medicine. We live in a society were new illnesses, and diseases have come from many different sources and mutated along the way. Therefore, western medicine, although tough on our bodies, is the only thing that will fight some of these illnesses quickly. We can heal ourselves, and you must believe that you can help yourself with many diseases and mental illnesses.

Become attuned to Reiki healing and then you can treat your child yourself and bring a balance to their meridians by purging out these toxins from their bodies. For those of you who have not experienced a Reiki session, you need to do so, as this is the way forward for alternative medicine. My only worry is that, as with everything, lots of people now call themselves Reiki Masters. But some have gained these certificates online, or from people who do not really know what they are doing, which is wrong. Dr Usui did not bring this incredible gift to us to be abused. Dr Usui was a scholar and a teacher who was born in Japan. He had watched the suffering in his village and wanted to help. I believe he was given this gift from heaven, giving him the ability to with the laying on of hands pass the universal energy through to those in need. He named this reiki. You can find his story if you google him.

It is meant to be attuned to you by a real person, a practising Reiki Master who lives within those energies, who stands in front of you and delivers the attunement as Dr Usui did many years ago. There are those people who are out for a quick buck, so you must do your homework, but there are many wonderful Reiki Masters who work within the light, who only have one thing in mind, your well-being, and that the attunement is delivered to you properly. You can visit my website for further details on attunement's.

Reiki and other holistic methods have been tried and tested over many centuries. I have seen great results from regular treatments, and I have included some success stories later in this book. If you teach your child to have holistic treatments regularly, then they will become used to this in their lives. This will show them how to self-heal and how to balance their own energy system, their chakras. Make this a part of their lives from the minute they are born to teach them the old ways, and they will pass on those teachings to their own children, and a new pattern will form.

In the following chapters of this book, you will read some real-life stories about young children and adults who have become clients of mine, usually through their parent coming to visit me first. During their visits, the Guides show me that there is a problem at home with the child and ask me to invite this child for a Reiki healing, or even a spiritual connection. Of course, each child is accompanied by their parent.

I feel that is one of the reasons I live the life I do; I believe that I am here to help children who are on the edge. This was confirmed to me once in a channelling session completed by a lady called Janet, who channelled a man named Zach. He told me that this was my life purpose and that I would guide the children back, show them the way and help them to realise who they are and why they are here.

Just to recap, the Star Children are moving into our hearts and are beginning to change and upgrade our long-time stagnant energy system. They are here to open our hearts and help us to claim our own spiritual power. By doing this, we will anchor ourselves in the new energy grid of evolution. They are here to teach through us to honour our planet and heal what has happened on Earth over hundreds of years. The outcome will be immense; this generation will stand up to the money makers of this world! And they will be heard! This planet is in danger of extinction, so listen and do not take a back seat. Start today and change something imperative to the existence of mankind and animal kind. Look out for these wonderfully evolved little humans because they are the future!

Our DNA Shutdown

YES! This sounds as crazy as a box of frogs but here goes!

Over the past twelve months, and on beginning to write this book, I have been told by higher masters that we are not running on full throttle. It is funny, but the way I was feeling as a human was shouting that out to me and very loudly! My Guide has channelled many things to me, but this channelling made such perfect sense.

In January 2019, after much grief and many losses in 2018, I took extremely ill with pneumonia. I am generally such a strong woman and very rarely catch a cold from the children. But it was Christmas 2018 and it hit me like a tonne of bricks. My body shut down and could not cope with what was happening. After ten months of weight loss, fatigue, anaemia, coughing, pain, and general ill health, I managed to pull through. To say it had been a tough year was an understatement, but I am, as my mum would say, still here to tell the story.

The funny thing is that my Spirit Guides have a strange way of giving me space to think, to write, and to listen to them. This was one of those times, and I felt so exhausted during those ten months that listening and writing was not high on my list of things to do.

My Guide and friend Zach have helped me through many heartaches and many losses over the past years. Zach stayed close to me over this time of illness, reassuring me that all would be fine. Some of my losses have not been deaths but have been friends that have backed away from me since my mum passed away. Strange, I know, as we usually turn to our friends when we lose someone so close to us. Both Zach and Clara, my Spirit Guides whom you will have read about in previous books, have told me that for these people to back away is a sign of weakness in their character, not mine. It is also weird how others can walk away from someone who needs a shoulder to lean on. But this happens, and as Zach would say, they are not meant to be here, their journey, whatever that may be, is not a part of my mission in this life.

It can be a very lonely life when you are walking that spiritual pathway, but I am so blessed with many kind and loving friends who have stood by me and helped me through bad times, just as I have done with them. We all have our cross to bear in this life, and if we can reach out and hold each other up when there is a need, then we are kind and caring souls.

As you have just read in the previous chapter, I also look after my son, who suffers from anxiety of the worst kind, and he chooses not to go out of our home, which can be hard for us as parents. My husband is an army veteran and is also in a bad way as he has seventeen damaged discs in his back and neck. This causes him daily pain and low mood, and he also has PTSD. Therefore, I felt I had to write this book. None of us has it easy in this life, but it would help if we were working at full throttle instead of a small percentage of what we need to survive.

Over the past months, Zach and Clara have been talking to me about our DNA. I must admit that this was a subject that went right over my head before they explained it to me, and I would never have understood what it was all about. I know that science has its account, but now you are going to hear about what the Spirit Guides say about the whole mess!

I was told that for years we, as humans, have been working on only two active physical strands of DNA. We also have a further ten energetic DNA strands which have been dormant within the Human Being for centuries. I had many questions during these sessions with my Guides. One of them was - why, if we are capable of so much more, is our DNA asleep?

After some research, I realised that the scientific world knows that these strands are lying dormant, and although I am far from a scientist, I imagine they are working tirelessly trying to find out why. But I feel our spirit teachers and masters have the answer. The effects of this loss are that we live in a spiritually damaged society, and our intuitive and healing abilities have been massively reduced. It has also resulted in us only accessing and using a tiny part of our brains. It is like turning your laptop on and finding only a small percentage of that laptop working. As you can imagine, this would cause problems through the rest of the system, and this is precisely what has been happening.

As a child, we arrive into the world with a vast knowledge of the higher energies who guide us daily. These Guides are the Angels, our spirit teams, and all the teachers that came before us. The human body is the most precious thing we will ever own. It stores and holds a large quantity of intelligence, wisdom, and knowledge on every aspect of ourselves, our world and all of life. Combinations of information are stored within the human brain, and a significant amount of data is stored inside the body. At conception, we receive, from our parents, specifically matched and paired recessive genes, our DNA map. These genes hold light codes that give us the chance to connect and develop our Spiritual abilities and for healing the damaged and wounded aspects of our Soul.

So consequently, if most of our DNA system is shut down, then we are struggling to connect to our true higher self. Some of us know that we are being called upon for higher good and over centuries this has come across as slightly wacky! Some of us hold that light within our souls and work daily to release the rest of our spiritual self from the DNA prison. Some teachers will help you to reactivate your twelve strands of DNA, and these people are connected to far more intelligent forms of energy than are here on Earth, that is for sure.

Awakening your DNA is a slow process, but as this re-configuration begins to work, we will create a more advanced nervous system that enables new information to move forward into our consciousness. The lightworkers are working with many of us, helping us to channel the healing of the DNA. This means that many of our dormant brain cells are awakening, and we will soon be able to access our full body capability.

As our bodies fill with more light, so our memories are opened, and as we evolve and as our DNA grows, we will become conscious Multidimensional Beings.

From where I am sitting this is all extremely exciting, and I am told that 2020 will be the time of ascension, and the people I am working closely with can also feel the shift. My groups have made immense progress in their ascension, and they can feel the difference in their bodies. Many, over the centuries, have looked upon people like me as strange, weird beings and some have been called evil and witches, especially by the Church.

Lightworkers are good souls who are trying to spread the light into this dark world. Yes, we are seen as a little strange, but this makes me smile because now it is becoming apparent that many are looking towards the lightworkers' way and towards the light energy from which we were all born.

To begin to heal our DNA, we must firstly look at our consumption. I asked what has caused people to close, to only be working on a small amount of what we are capable of, and this was the answer.

Over hundreds of years, we as humans have been so desperate to improve everything around us, better electricity, different types of fuels, faster food, instant this and instant that, we have created a monster! If you take yourself back just a hundred years, life was much more straightforward. The meat was grown by the farmer in beautiful pastureland, chickens roamed free and laid fresh, disease-free eggs, all of which was gathered and put into the corner shop for that day's trade. Nothing went through huge factories or big conglomerates of supermarkets. No one else controlled our diet - we did! Everything was personal and fresh, and the milk was delivered every morning by the farmer who had milked the cow.

These days we have such a lot of fast food, even the supermarkets' shelves are just full to busting with tinned goods and ready meals. This fast food is so bad for us, and humanity has become lazy and weak because of this food. I have heard many say that food is food, but this is not true. I have learnt from the Spirit Guides that the food we consume is controlled by vast conglomerates of people who are making money from our ill health, and from obesity, the disease that is now taking over the world! Then there is the bleach smell in our water, the high consumption of salt and preservatives, I could go on, but I think you get the picture. It all must stop! And the only way to do this is for us as individuals to take the lead. Stop feeding our children crap! This is shutting down our systems, our live DNA. It is causing our gifted children to have minimal use of their brain and their potential. None of us would intentionally hurt our children, but they follow our lead like sheep do. We must start to make decisions for ourselves, filter our tap water, stop buying supermarket rubbish, everyone must take responsibility for their actions, and we need to do this now.

I have been working as a Reiki Master for some years now, and I have found that a lot of mental illness and indeed, physical illness is trapped within our energy systems, our chakras. For those of you who have had a Reiki session, you will know that you leave feeling lighter and calmer.

This is because while you are with us, we are clearing away any negative energy that has piled up and caused blockages. To clear our chakras, we must realign, activate, and connect our twelve strands of DNA to our twelve Chakra points, which are our energy doorways through which we access our Spiritual heritage. The twelve strands of DNA serve as links through the twelve chakras to the energy web outside of our bodies. The twelve chakras act as energetic doorways into our body, connecting us to the vital forces of existence. It is through opening and activating these portals of energy that we can begin to truly know ourselves. The higher powers are working now with lightworkers like myself here on Earth to do this job. As all twelve strands of DNA are now forming, whatever issues we have not dealt with and peacefully cleared in our personal history, will create chaos. Feelings and memories are emerging, offering us an opportunity to experience the fabric of our being and revealing who we are through the events and beliefs that are intricately woven into us.

We all need to take responsibility and do it now! Start Reiki sessions or learn how to heal yourself. Deal with what you are eating or drinking and buy good things that you know are fresh and not processed. Start small - buy a water filter jug and use that instead of bottled water. Make a stand today, and buy fresh veg, cook home-cooked meals, buy from a farmer, not the supermarket. Cut out sugars and see how you feel within the month. Go back to basics and remember that although we are controlled by governments and the hierarchy of world leaders, we can make a stand now!

Unprecedented Times

The Forgotten was written mid to late 2019 and was due to be published March 2020. However, I find myself confined to my home in isolation due to the outbreak of COVID-19, the Corona Virus. I have no means of getting my book out to the world as my editor has been gravely ill after heart surgery. You could not write this shit could you!

My spirit guides are driving me nuts, they are pushing me to do it myself! The book has received two edits from people who too are authors. They have gone through the book with a fine-tooth comb, and so here I am in an unfamiliar place, about to self-publish my fourth book! And terrified at the thought of doing so!

Over the past 48 hours, I have had thoughts running through my mind of how accurate everything I had written in the previous chapters has become.

It is Tuesday 31st March 2020, and we as a family are now 14 days into our self-isolation. I have been trying to keep up online with as much help as I can offer for those who are stressed and anxious over this world lockdown. I find it all somewhat surreal to be honest. It is like a well-written script from a sci-fi movie. Where countries were infiltrated by deadly viruses and people had to flee to their homes to stay safe!

My book is finished, or is it? I decided to give the chapters a final read before deciding whether I was brave enough to venture into the self-publishing world. On doing so, I realised that a significant gap had formed in my book over the past month. After putting all the chapters together, I knew that this was the intervention of my spirit guides. So, I set forth to write what was now becoming incredibly clear.

On writing this new chapter, I have dusted down some of the meditations and group recordings which were made starting as far back as 2018 -2019. During these meditations which are channeled to me by guides, you can hear them telling the group of something big that is coming in 2020. These recordings reveal of a colossal spiritual shift that will happen in the spring! On listening back to the recordings, I realise that this lockdown across the world was what we were being warned about. I just had not grasped that sadly humanity would come its knees for this healing of mother earth to happen.

There were many meditations during this time and many channelings within these four walls to my trusted group. We were being brought back to shamanic times where the Earth was honored and worshipped as a sacred place. We were taught how to protect ourselves and to prepare for what was about to happen.

For many years we trusted our guides and were shown how to stay grounded, we did this by sending our roots down into mother earth and asking her to keep us grounded and safe. It was around October 2019, and we were all feeling fatigued, and our energies were lower than ever before. It was during a session of the group on a Tuesday night that my guides spoke out and completely changed how we should do our grounding. I am not going to lie to you, we were all slightly taken back by this sudden urge to change this.

Usually, we would see our roots tunneling down into mother earth holding onto the great tree roots and weathering all storms. We had grounded ourselves like this for years, but now it had to stop when I asked why Zach told me it was in preparation of what was to come. We were being asked to see a bubble forming around us starting at our feet and closing in a complete circle above our crowns. Then we were asked to fill that bubble with a blinding white light, this is the light of creation. With immediate effect, our energy levels were lifted, and we started to feel well again. It was a miracle every member of the group was lifted. I would ask each one of you reading my book to try this out its amazing.

As the guide came into the room to bring us this message, he told us that every single one of us could receive divine inspiration. That is why we were chosen, he told us to meditate on the true meaning of "love," and to open our heart's, soul, and mind, and it will come.

During these meditations, we were lifted by angel's, lifted out of the room and into Earth's atmosphere. The sight to behold was unbelievable, the sky was full of stars. These stars filled the sky like tiny diamonds glistening and bright. It was the promise of life in the darkness, a sense of warmth springing from the cold. It was a vastness to bring humbleness and an eternal space to bring gratitude for the cosiness of home. Knowing that if we were taken high and out of Earth's atmosphere, we would feel more connected to those far away stars, perhaps sensing the vulnerability of Earth even more. We could see the galaxy of planets all around us, the aurora lights come as nature's carnival dance. They flowed over the sky in brilliant waves. It is as if God wrote "hope" in the sky with electric-neon crayons and asked them to dance. Whether you believe in God or not now was not the time to question his existence. It was breathtakingly beautiful, and we had never felt more alive than at this moment, floating in space and time with the angels.

We could see other beings all around us, lightworkers as my guide calls us. Everyone gleamed like a bright beam of light. Lightworkers came from every nation, every planet, every colour skin both man woman and child, were present up there up in the starlit sky.

We were asked to join hands and form a solid ring of light around the world, like a golden halo. As we did this another ring formed behind us a solid gold ring. In this second ring, we could see our teachers and our spirit guides, it was quite a remarkable sight to behold. We were suspended in space, no one felt anxious we felt safe and surrounded by love. A third ring began to form behind the teachers and guides, we felt quite emotional as the third ring was all the angels, they were magnificent. They spread their wings to form the third circle around the world.

We could see the brightest light of all was coming from the centre; this was Archangel Raphael and Archangel Michael. We could also see the light of Christ within this circle, and the view was utterly amazing.

We were instructed to send a beam of healing out towards the planet, this beam of light came straight from our hearts. This was one of the most moving and extraordinary meditations we had ever done, we could feel the power in the energies of like-minded people. It was very humbling to be a part of this remarkable healing that was taking place.

As I brought the group back from the meditation, I could see their faces were filled with astonishment. They all glanced at each other and simultaneously asked, "what just happened?"

It took us a while to compose ourselves as the energies were high in the room. Each of the group spoke separately about their experience, what they felt, and what they had seen, it was, well just out of this world! Literally!

We were told that we were being called upon as lightworkers and that it would all become apparent. As a group, we worked hard last year listening to the teachers and doing as we were instructed, which was to bring light to a planet that was darkening by the day. We were shown the world being raped, for want of a better word! The sea's beginning to die, the forests burning, people starving in a world of plenty and much more.

It was a very upsetting thing to witness, but the lightworkers in my groups took it well and chose to keep beaming that love and light out there. Greed had overtaken our planet, those who were wealthy beyond their wildest dreams just wanted more. Country leaders were living in palaces while the poor lived on the streets, hungry cold and unloved. While sitting at their golden tables were filled with plenty, their citizens starved and were so weak, they ate vermin to survive.

There are many different theories out there to how the COVID-19 came to be. How it has consumed our planet and taking many souls with it, but it all boils down to greed no matter which theory you choose to believe. We live in a world of plenty, and the desire for more has brought this planet to its knees. The devil is in the details was a message I received.

This morning, as I said earlier, I am 14 days into isolation, I have been meditating with my spirit guides, Clara, and Zach. I know I have had this conversation with a couple of you. Still, I wanted to share my findings. I am in a fantastic place spiritually I can feel the enormous shift that is happening all around me. The world is awakening, and the healing energies and the angelic presence is remarkable, it brings me to tears. I have always felt so blessed to share my world with these teachers and the angelic realms, but their presence now is overflowing.

The world's population is in utter chaos, but Mother Earth is doing her happy dance. This is what all of us Earth angels have been sensing for many years. It is so beautiful amongst the stress of the outside world. Without getting too biblical, I have taught for many years that the light we see is the light of creation, the Christ energy. Sadly, we all know, and we can feel at times the other side of life, its darkness, its dark side, the devil if you want to call it that.

In a pandemic, the negative chaos can become deadlier than the virus. Especially if the virus is killing those who would have soon died in any case - as much as we love them and wish to protect them. I spoke in my previous books about our contract of life which we agreed upon before we were born. We all have our date and time that we will pass back over to the spirit world, and this will happen no matter what the cause.

Life can be lost from violence or deterioration of health in mental and physical terms. Seeing all the potential avenues for saving people is paramount. And so, in addition to ramping up healthcare provision and slowing the numbers of infected people to a manageable flow, an essential way to save people is social order and the following of rules. So, we follow the rules, and we do this from a sense of love for one another. It's not that I help you and you help me; instead, I help him, you help her, and because we all do that, there is help for us all. We all have skills and areas of need, and when our ability matches the needs of another, there is the most beautiful feeling of joy. We find an opportunity to help! That is a community, and it's incredible.

To promote peace, to prevent war, to bring societal health, we must reverse the artificial shortages of essential resources around the world. Food suppression must end, the technological advances that can bring an age of abundance, must be developed for the benefit of the entire species, in the spirit of cooperation and love and not developed, despite the damage to our health.

The Christ energies have been so prominent over the past ten years or more. So, our lightworkers, Zach and Clara and many more have been preparing us for what was to come. We are experiencing some unprecedented times now that is for sure, and as humans, it is scary. But as lightworkers are being called upon to shine brighter than ever before.

I feel everyone's pain and worry, I genuinely do. Still, I want you to know that Zach and Clara and many others are reaching out to you all today and asking that you join them in lifting our world back up. Planet Earth just could not take any more, people have been worried that our planet would die, but the frightening truth is that Mother Earth will survive and is fighting back. She will confine us to our homes, stop us from clearing her forests and killing the animals and the fish. She will clear the skies of airplanes and let the world breathe again if only for a while. It is as if she has shut us down while she does her work. For many centuries there has been no blue sky over Beijing. Their air has been polluted, and poisonous smog has filled the lungs of both humans and the planet. As the world begins to heal pollution has lifted over Beijing, and that part of our planet breathes again.

Dolphins are feeding in rivers and jumping for joy at the peace that has now come to the seas.

World leaders have taken control of all resources and pushed us aside. As lightworkers, we are protected, and I want you to believe this, bring your light energy up high, stay positive and breathe. As a teacher, I am here trying to help you to understand the channellings. As a friend, I love you all dearly, and we will stand together again when the light stands strong over this darkness.

The world is awakening the light will triumph over the devil! But we must all do our part, the question is, are we listening, has Mother Earth shouted loud enough?

The following chapters are true accounts from my client's time with me in my healing rooms. There stories are both touching and powerful, and for sharing them with us I am grateful.

Mike

It was some years ago, well before Christmas 2017, that I had received a text message for a booking. The man gave his first name as Mike, and when I asked him what he would like to book for, and he replied, "Anything that will help me."

I called him for a quick chat, and he told me that he was so worried that he did not know where his life was going, and he didn't know what else to do. I could hear the panic in his voice, so I asked him to first come for a healing session and suggested that we take it from there.

We were booked in for the end of November 2017, but when the morning of Mike's appointment came, Mike did not. I had a feeling that morning that he wasn't going to show for his appointment. I had messaged him the night before, as I do with all my clients, and he had replied telling me he was still attending.

There was something in his voice when we spoke earlier to make the booking, that told me he was not going to attend. But he sounded desperate, so I booked him in hoping that he would be brave enough to come. It was about fifteen minutes after he should have arrived that my phone pinged. The message read, "I am terribly sorry, I got as far as the lighthouse and froze, I just couldn't do it. I feel so stupid. Why do I bother to even get up in the morning? What kind of man am I?"

I was in the middle of texting him back, when my phone pinged again, and the message read, "A weak one!" He was answering his own question.

I called him immediately and asked him where he was now. He told me he was standing on the seafront staring out to sea.

"Stay right there," I told him. "I will be with you in two minutes."

This was an unusual thing for me to do, as I didn't even know this man, we had only spoken on the telephone. So, I grabbed my coat, told my husband where I was going, and I headed up to the seafront.

It was a freezing cold day; winter was undoubtedly setting in. As I reached the top of the embankment, I could see the top of a man's head. He was dressed very smartly in a dark grey suit.

"Mike, is that you?" I asked. He turned around sharply as if I had startled him. He just nodded. I took one look at his face and could tell that he had been crying. He looked lost, and he looked cold. I would say Mike looked about sixty-five years old, with sad eyes as if the light had gone out in his soul. It was as if time stopped for a moment, and that moment gave me the time to assess this broken-looking man standing in front of me.

"Are you okay?" I asked. "You look freezing cold."

"Not really," he replied with tears in his eyes. "Excuse the state of me. It's windy up here, and it makes my eyes run something terrible."

I just smiled, as I knew that those were tears of sadness that I could see running down his face.

"Come on," I said. "It's blinking Baltic up here. I don't know about you, but I could do with a cuppa."

Mike smiled, picked up his overcoat, which was lying on the wall, and followed me down the hill towards my house. As I reached the house, I could see my husband watching out of the window, and I mouthed the words *put the kettle* on to him. As we stepped in through the doorway, Mike took off his shoes immediately. "What a gentleman," I thought as I showed him down to my lovely workroom.

As he stepped inside the room, he paused. "Wow!" he gasped, and stood there, taking in the atmosphere in the room.

"What is that feeling in here?" His eyes were filling up fast again. "A feeling of complete and utter peace, as if someone had just lifted a bag of potatoes off my shoulders. The most remarkable feeling I have ever felt." He smiled

"That will be the Angels," I replied. "They all arrived for the day, early this morning."

Mike turned and looked at me with a look on his face that I had seen many times before from people who thought that standing before them was a slightly crazy lady with a vivid imagination!

There came a tap on the door, and it was my husband with our lovely hot tea.

Mike and I sat and chatted for a while, and as we did so, I could see the Angels around him, bringing him comfort. A funny thing had happened that morning. When I awoke, I only had three people booked in for that day, one after the other, and two of them were coming together. Yes, you guessed it, they had cancelled at the last minute. This left me with a lot of time on my hands to try and gain Mike's trust. We sat and had our cup of tea and just chatted informally as if we had known each other for years. Mike had a lovely personality; he cracked the odd joke and smiled a lot while he was with me that day. While we were chatting, I was picking up messages from my

Guides and throwing the odd thing into the conversation to help him to speak out and confide in us.

I was being told that this man was on the edge and that I was his last resort. The Guides showed me a man in the spirit world, and I wasn't sure if I should tell Mike, but I was pushed to do so.

"I know you haven't come here for connection to a loved one, or a glimpse into your future, but as you must know, I am a medium. I sense others who have passed away."

He gazed at me, tears again welling up in his eyes.

"I don't want to upset you, but I have a man here. The feeling I get is that he is a father figure. Am I okay to bring him in? It feels he has things he needs to tell you."

Mike just nodded without saying a word. He stared straight at me, as if wondering what on Earth was going to happen next.

Those of you who have had readings with me and had connections to your loved ones will know that I am quite a strong clairsentient, so this means I can use this to my advantage. I ask your loved ones to show me how they passed away, so that the client knows without a doubt that this is their loved one who is with us and I am not just making it up as I go along.

The Angels pushed this man forward, and I could feel pain coming from him. I had no sense in my usual way of how he had passed away. It was as if he was blocking his death from me, but I have sensed this before, and it usually turned out to be an unfortunate death. I could feel his energy, which I had felt before, many times from those with anxiety, or in a state of panic. In my head, I asked my Guides to help me, as I wasn't picking up much at all from this spirit. Within an instant, the message came back from the Guides, "He must show you himself, Lynn. This is a part of his transition into spirit. We all must accept life as we knew it, in death."

I talked to Mike and described the spirit I had with me. I told him how I was feeling pure love coming from this man, but there was also an element of shame. The energy I could feel was a young one, I would say around eighteen, but it was strange because the energy kept on changing, to an older man closer to the age of forty to forty-five. I told all of this to Mike with a confused look on my face, and he just stared at me in disbelief. I knew this man was Mike's father; I had felt that energy so many times before. I told him this and said to him that for some reason, his father wanted to be eighteen years old again. I asked Mike if this made sense.

Mike nodded, so I continued. In my mind, I was trying to converse with the spirit of Mike's dad, and I was telling him that he needed to show me how he had passed over, no matter how painful it was. I told him that Mike needed him now and that it was time to put things straight.

Suddenly, I felt very cold as if I had been plunged into freezing water. I felt myself gasp. "Wow has it gone cold in here or is it just me? I feel like I have just jumped into an ice-cold bath."

The cold felt intense. Mike looked straight into my eyes, and as the tears began to flow rapidly down his face, he said to me, "You do have my dad. You really do have my dad."

I could feel the ice-cold water all around me, so I continued to speak out loud to Mike and tell him everything I was feeling. I felt that his father had drowned, and I felt as if I was surrounded by the sea. I also realised why this man hadn't wanted to show me how he had passed away. Because I am afraid of the water, I do feel that I was drowned in another life. So, this gentle spirit was trying not to make me live through something that terrified me!

It was just at that moment, somewhere between me quietly panicking to myself, and Mike staring into me as if he couldn't believe what he heard, that he spoke out.

"It is my dad. You have my dad," he said again with tears running down his face.

Mike sobbed while he told me how his dad had taken his own life, how he had plunged himself into the sea in darkness and wasn't found until the next tide. Listening to this nearly brought me to tears, but I was holding my breath and trying to be strong for my client.

The other feeling that I had from his dad was of a very anxious man. I had voiced this earlier to Mike, and so he continued to tell me about his dad and their life. I could see his father dressed very smartly, but I also kept seeing him in some sort of uniform. I continued to tell Mike all I could feel and see, and he kept confirming all that I was saying. I felt his father had been to war at some time, and this had caused him significant trauma. Although he loved his family, he did not cope with life after the war. He had seen and done some terrible things for his country, and this had sent him plummeting into what he described as HELL! Back in the early 1900s, men were men; they didn't speak of anxiety or depression, they just got on with life and worked hard for their families and quietly died inside.

My heart was breaking listening to Mike, and his father both describe their lives and how extremely hard it was at times. Mike's father spoke of how deeply sorry he was to have caused such sadness in his only son. I was told by Mike of his father's struggle with life and how he lived an empty life once he had come home from the war. He had gone to battle as a young man, in fact, he was just about old enough to be recruited into the army, as they gathered up the troops and took them off to war. Mike's father's life would never be the same; he went away a happy lad and came home a broken soldier.

He had met a young woman, a nurse, while away at war. She understood the trauma that he was enduring, and so was the perfect match for him. They were soon married and had a child. Mike had grown up a happy little boy but had watched his father lock himself away at times due to stress and anxiety. This, of course, was not diagnosed in those days; people just had to live with their illness and hope that their families understood. Mike's mum looked after the child and the house and had part-time work to make ends meet because her husband had a lot of time off work due to this invisible illness. He had very few friends, and they didn't socialise at all; life was quite a lonely one for the family.

Of course, Mike knew no different - this was his life, and at the age of four, he started school. This was an excellent place for him to be because he met new children and made some friends. He loved his classwork and was quite the academic. This also meant that his mother had a little time to breathe at home, as life was full-on.

The family lived in New Brighton on the Wirral. Mike and his mother spent many happy times sitting on the warm sands just looking out to sea. His father worked at Cammell Lairds shipyard, or at least he did so when he could manage to get out of the house. As a child growing up, if you haven't mixed with many families, you begin to believe that this is how everyone's life is.

Mike was now seven years old, and he had gone off to school like any other day. He hadn't seen his father since the previous day as he was in bed before he had arrived home from work. It was winter and the day was cold. The school bell rang, and all the children left the classroom to go find their mothers in the playground. When Mike reached the yard, the lady who lived next door to them was standing there waiting for him. She told him that his mum had to go on a message, and she was to take him home until his mother returned.

The truth was somewhat different. Mike's father had not come home the night before and was not in the house that day as Mike went to school. His father's life had become so painful that as he walked home along the seafront from his work at the docks, he just stood looking out to sea. In his mind he felt useless and broken, he could take no more and sat and wrote a note to his family, placed it inside his sandwich tin, left the tin on the bench at the edge of the sea, then plunged himself into the ice-cold water and was not seen alive again.

As this story unfolded, I could see the torment on Mike's face. No wonder his father didn't want to show me how he passed away. The ice-cold water I could feel around me was the sea, and the torment I could feel was his father's state of mind.

Mike never understood where his dad had gone or why; he loved him so very much. Their world had fallen apart. Mike's dad had been suffering from PTSD, which of course, these days is diagnosed as a disorder. Back when Mike was a child, it was just called shell shock, and little help, if any, was given to the patient.

Well, things haven't changed much sixty-five years later! It is time our country stepped up to the plate as we hear of too many suicides just on the Wirral.

Mike's father said he was sorry, asked his son's forgiveness and then left us to continue our session. Sitting with Mike for over an hour now, I could see the signs of his own anxiety and PTSD. He was sweating and wringing his hands as he sat there, and although he was quite charming and always smiling, behind his eyes was pain and suffering. I was exhausted by this time, as the stressful energy in the room was quite something to bear when you are an empath.

I talked some time about the benefits of Reiki Healing, but Mike just sat and stared at me. I asked him what his beliefs were, and that's when I realised just how bad this man's mental state was.

He told me that he had been to many therapists and grief counsellors, and he had paid for them all privately; he had seen many different doctors, but he still felt in such a desperate state.

It was at that moment one of my Guides told me to ask him a question.

"Mike, may I ask you something?" I asked. Mike nodded. "A while ago when I found you up on the embankment by the sea, what was going through your mind?"

Mike stared at me, with no answer.

"I ask this because meeting you up there was out of character for me. I don't usually go running out of my nice warm house to meet clients on the ice-cold seafront. But when you texted me, my Guides told me you were desperate and encouraged me to come and find you. When I found you, the sea was bashing on the rocks at your feet, and it was the coldest day ever. But you had taken off your overcoat and laid it down on the wall. You were standing there with your feet wet from the splashes of the sea." There was still no response from him, apart from the tears coursing down his face.

My heart was beating fast at this point, so I knew that I was on the right track as I spoke. I tried to lighten the conversation by making a joke about the situation.

"I hope you weren't thinking of going for a swim in that cold sea," I smiled. "That would have really ruined my day, as I can't swim, so who would have saved you?"

Mike smiled as he looked up. He told me that he had been standing there at the water's edge for fifteen minutes. He also told me how he had prayed for help and prayed that the Angels would come and take him. I felt my heart sink. How sad this all was. Then he wiped his tears away from his eyes, and said, "And there she was. An Angel had come to rescue me. God had answered my prayers. I was about to walk into that cold sea just as you stepped up onto the embankment, and you smiled at me and greeted me like a long-lost friend. I knew at that moment that you had come to save me."

I smiled at Mike and said, "Well you know I have seen many things I cannot explain over the years, and I believe that you truly had your prayers answered today, my friend, because that was the first time I felt I needed to come and find one of my clients. I have never had the urge to run out into the cold on a November's morning."

"Thank you, thank you so much. You have a beautiful way about you Lynn, and I feel for the first time in many years I am safe. I can try and move forward."

I told Mike of the benefits of Reiki healing and how it helps immensely with anxiety. He sat and listened to me tell him of some small miracles that had happened during these healings, and how I believe wholeheartedly that everyone can receive some benefit from it.

"It all sounds a little like hocus pocus to me," he said.

"Are you kidding me? After all that has happened today, you're telling me that a Reiki healing is hocus pocus?" I laughed out loud. "That's the least of the hocus pocus you have witnessed today."

Mike laughed too and agreed that this day had turned out quite different from how he expected it to when he awoke this morning.

He agreed to have Reiki from me right there and then. The session was very calming and brought energy into the room that made us all feel calm and free. Mike enjoyed every minute of it and told me that he hadn't felt that relaxed for many years.

We agreed that Reiki was the way forward and we block-booked over the next couple of months. Mike came weekly to see me every Wednesday afternoon on his half-day from work. I watched him evolving and coming out from his shell and into a man who stood strong and tall. It was a pleasure to help him. He was a beautiful person inside and out. It is now two years later, and his weekly sessions have turned to once every two months. He is re-married to a lovely lady who adores him, his business has grown immensely, and balance has been restored in his life.

A broken man who was about to commit suicide came through my door on that cold November morning, and now nearly two years later, he is happy and living a healthy life. If that is not a healing miracle, I don't know what is. Sadly, Mike lost his mum in 2018; she died peacefully in her sleep at the age of 91. She had all her marbles (his words, not mine), and died in peace knowing that her son was recovering from a lifetime of torture caused by anxiety and PTSD. I thought this might have pushed him over the edge again, but he increased his sessions back to once a week until the anxiety had retreated.

Of course, anxiety lives in every one of us, but currently, it is becoming very prominent in many people. No, Reiki healing doesn't cure everything or everyone, as that would upset the balance in the world. However, it helps in such a positive way to bring calm and peace into many lives. I feel it is so much harder for a man to admit a mental illness; I have seen it all too often, but I want you to know that I can help. The first step is to knock on my door, share a cup of tea, and then you realise that I am okay, and you can trust your time with me to be healing.

I believe that although a very private man, Mike will continue to be a part of the Reiki Healing circle in this crazy world we live in and I thank the God and his Angels for bringing his lost soul to me on that cold winter's day.

The Invisible Lady

It was around 2017 when I was contacted by a lady who, to protect her identity, we will call Karen. Karen contacted me by text message asking if I could send her some distance Reiki. She told me that she had been scouring the Internet, looking for someone who she felt she could trust to help her heal. I called her up on the phone, but she did not answer, so we continued our chat by text message. This was quite difficult as it can take a while to text in detail.

But we managed fine, and through the text, I found out a little about this lady called Karen. Even though we didn't speak to each other, I could feel the sadness coming from a lost human being, and it was a sadness I knew too well. There was a lot of reading between the lines that had to be done, as there were things she had not told me. Karen continued with the texts telling me that she was in a lot of pain in many areas of her life. It was sad to hear that she had not left the house in many years due to anxiety and the fear of being amongst other human beings. Some of Karen's pain was also physical because she suffered from extremely painful eczema, which flared up when she was stressed or anxious. She also had a lot of pain which radiated from her hips and into her legs, which in her words, at times floored her.

I explained who I was and how I worked and agreed I would send distance Reiki healing to her, and so it began, a relationship with an invisible lady. There were times when Karen would insist on paying me for my time, and there other were times when I declared I would be sending the healing as a gift from one human being to another.

I messaged her on the days I would send the healing and explained the process to her so that she could participate in her own healing. I told her that she was to find a quiet place, and if possible, to lie down, close her eyes and focus on her breathing, as the healing was coming to her in the form of divine energy.

I used to do this around 9-10pm, so often I never heard from Karen until the next day as she had fallen asleep during the healing. This, of course, was fabulous as a part of her trauma was not sleeping at night and then feeling exhausted during the day. This was a pattern that had flowed through her life for many years. The following day I always received a text message telling me that the energies were beautiful, and that Karen slept very well that night, and the texts repeatedly ended, *thank you so much*.

I would call in the Reiki Masters and the Angels, and just before I began the healing, I would feel my bedroom filled with their fantastic energy. My room seemed to glimmer like moonlight, pale blue in colour, and it was such a beautiful feeling of peace and calm. After I had finished the healings, I would thank them and within minutes fall fast asleep. There were times when I would wake up a few hours later and my room was still glistening as if there was a candle burning. But of course, there wasn't, it was the Angels, who had stayed with me to help me to sleep. I always felt so fortunate to be receiving such loving attention, and every day I am grateful.

Week in and week out for nearly two years, I chatted by text and sent distance healing to a lady I had never met. I had a considerable amount of compassion for her as I had seen anxiety and what it had done to my own son. Although she never heard my voice, or so I thought, she connected with me in such a way that it brought her immense peace and stillness in her stressful life. I began to add Karen to the healing energies which we sent out on a Monday and Tuesday after my development groups. Within the group, and because of the presence of the Angels and our teachers, the most magnificent energy would grow in the room.

Sometimes it was quite breath-taking; the room at the end of the evening felt as if it would burst open from the energies surging around us, so I thought that it was a beautiful thing to share with the Universe, as there was so much love in that room. We would give thanks to our teachers that night, and I would guide the group into gathering the energies up and sending them into the Universe. While doing this, I would ask the Angels to take every spark of loving energy and place it into the hearts of those who were desperate or ill. The members of the groups used to give me names of people they knew who were sick and we would ask for the energy to be sent to them first before we sent it out into the Universe. We included Karen in this method of sending healing. It was quite the feeling as you saw this energy in your third eye splash out across the night sky and knowing it was being delivered to those in need.

Karen told me that the energies coming from the group night was so magnificent that it brought her to tears on many occasions. I show gratitude daily for the love and energy from God and the Angels that is channelled through me in my groups. It is very humbling indeed to be a part of this process of healing the world.

Month in month out, year in year out, I sent this lovely soul Karen along with many others healing every week, never meeting her, not knowing even what she looked like, as she wouldn't send me a picture of herself.

Then suddenly, around May 2019, I received a text message from Karen. She was asking me if she could book for a reading and a Reiki session. I was not shocked by her request as the Angels had told me this day would come. However, for many years she had said that she could not come to me. Of course, I booked her in straight away, but I did wonder if she would come. She did, though. With her daughter as her chaperone, and with a smile on her lovely face, she walked through my door for the first time in over two years. I was so thrilled to meet her face to face at last.

I showed Karen to my room, and she smiled from ear to ear, she was so happy to be here. I told her we would give her Reiki first to help her to feel calm and relaxed. The session was remarkable; the Angels filled the room, the Reiki Masters stood beside me, and the energies were mind-blowing. I watched as Karen drew this amazing love and healing straight into her body and mind. She was glowing, and the room felt peaceful and calm.

We began her reading, and because I knew that Karen had not left her home for many years, I asked her what it was she wanted to know from her reading. She smiled and asked me to see if she would have her life back.

The reading was remarkable, and of course, Karen had things in her mind that she had not revealed to me. Her reading showed holidays that she had missed out on over the past years, it showed her being set free from the shackles in which she had been imprisoned over the years. These shackles were very real, and they indeed left their mark on Karen's body, in forms of circles of eczema around her ankles. It was quite extraordinary to be honest, as you would swear that this is what had happened to her and had left its mark. It even revealed Karen taking her driving lessons, which brought so much light into the room, as now Karen herself had begun to glow. She was the light, and she was shining for all to see.

Her session with me was very emotional for both of us as I also understood so well what it was she had been going through for so many years, the fear of other people, the pressure she felt society had put upon her, the fear of going outside, the way her heart would beat so fast that she thought she would die. All these are symptoms I had seen so many times in my loved ones. It saddened me indeed, but anxiety is something that is happening all around the world.

Now came the moment I will never forget, and it makes every heartache I have had to go through to write my books so very worthwhile. I asked Karen how she managed to come to see me after two years of not wanting to. Her reply brought tears to my eye.

"Lynn, I read your books, and your truth and honesty were astounding. The story of your battle with your son and his anxiety brought me to tears. I knew that this was me you were talking about; this was how I lived my life. I was at the end of my sanity, and I had no hope, you and your son saved my life. Through your own pain and sadness, and through your son's sheer determination, I am here. You gave me hope, and for that, I am eternally grateful."

I felt so emotional hearing Karen talk about my writing this way. I was so afraid to put such detail in my books, but I was later to find out that Karen wasn't the only soul who was set free from their shackles by my honesty.

Karen told me of her dreams to go on holiday without fear of keeling over with the pain of anxiety. She also told me that she would love to learn to drive and how she always thought this would be impossible. I smiled from ear to ear, listening to her tell me about her dreams. As our session came to an end, I asked her if she would be coming back, and she replied undoubtedly, "YES!"

It has only been weeks since Karen came to visit me, but I text her regularly, to ask her how she is doing.

I felt on top of the world that day. Who would have thought that my honest but straightforward account of our lives would have helped so many people? It is very humbling to know that sometimes our own fight can save another's life. When I wrote A Light to Guide us Home, I really didn't want to write it. I had my own reasons; I am a private person, and this book threw my life out there for all to see, but sometimes it is the right thing to do, and my Guides, Raoul and the Angels had to convince me that my chaotic life would save many others.

For those of you who have read my books, you know that my son was also in a bad place. I feel it is death that pushes my son over the edge. When his father died, his anxiety put him in prison, in the darkness of his own bedroom for five years. As you read his story, you will realise it wasn't easy to get him outside and trying to live life again. Unfortunately, the loss of his grandmother six months ago has pushed him right back into a dark place, and so the battle begins again.

For all of you reading The Forgotten, this book is for you, yes, I am talking directly to you! To all who suffer from the debilitating illness of anxiety and panic attacks and many other mental illnesses, or those who have family members who suffer with this darkness, I send to you hope and healing, love and understanding for all you are going through currently. May the Angels surround you with their healing light and may God put a bubble of love around you daily and keep you safe. I pray that where it is possible you can be delivered to me to be surrounded by the Angels who love you and want to help you to find the real you, the person who has been imprisoned inside your mind for far too long. You were born without stress and anxiety; you were born to be the best possible version of you. I wish you love and healing right now wherever you are.

Jess

I met Jess in 2018. She is the girlfriend of my grandson Joe, and I could see straight away that she was a quiet and quite an anxious girl. She would come to family parties or get-togethers and sit, observing all that was going on. Jess is a beautiful young lady and was only fourteen when I met her.

It was my daughter Nikki who told me of the extent of Jess's anxiety. Jess is a very clever girl but was struggling with her last years at school, and the sad thing is she wasn't on her own. There are many children and adults out there who suffer from the invisible mental illness of anxiety. Sometimes it's even hidden from their families. They seem happy and chatty at home, and all looks well, but in social circumstances, they fall to pieces inside.

Since my children were small, we have always had a family holiday every year, and as they grew up, they would bring girlfriends or boyfriends, then eventually they would begin to bring their own children. I have had many ask me if I am crazy as the numbers grew slowly, and gradually we went from a family of five, plus my mum, as she would also come with us every year until she got too old to cope with the crowd, to now a party of thirteen! I won't lie! At times, the noise is somewhat overwhelming, but how I love those holidays. They are my family, and those times have made such beautiful memories.

Jess came on many holidays with us. She always loved the children and really interacted with them well. She understood my granddaughter who has also been suffering from anxiety for most of her life, which is sad as she is only seven years old. Jess is always kind and courteous but is somewhat quiet and reserved. I recognised this, as it's been a hard twenty-six years for my son, who has been suffering from anxiety since he was two. I can understand why people look at Jess and think that perhaps she is rude because she does not interact with them, because this has happened with my granddaughter and my son on many occasions.

I can always tell when Jess is worried, because she stands very quietly with her arms crossed across her stomach and her eyes at a steady stare, as if she had just about holding it all in.

I knew straight away that Jess was suffering from anxiety; you could see in her lovely eyes. She absolutely loved to be around us with the positive energy and banter we had as a family. Jess loved coming on holiday with us. She felt relaxed; she had no problem at all. Jess ate with us, came to restaurants with us and felt safe in her surroundings. On reflection, I think that underneath she struggled a lot. It wasn't until she started to prepare for her exams in school that I saw this anxiety heighten in her. Jess had heard my grandchildren asking for magic from me on several occasions and always wondered what this was. They often asked me for what they called magic if they didn't feel very well.

Of course, it was Reiki that they were receiving. They always loved it and without a doubt, Reiki "magic" always helped them. Jess asked my daughter what it was that I was doing when I gave them magic. My daughter explained what it was and explained how it had helped many with anxiety.

Nikki sent me a message and asked if I would help Jess and told me of the extent of her anxiety. Of course, I said I would help, and Jess came to see me with her sister. Jess responded amazingly to the radiant energy of Reiki. It was the second time that Jess came to me she told me that her teacher had noticed the difference in her and had commented. Jess had told her teacher that she was coming to me and that it had helped her a lot. This teacher was a considerable support for Jess and told her that during the exams period, she could use her free lessons to attend a Reiki treatment.

Sometimes her mum would drop her off, and she would just have half an hour of Reiki, which would calm her nerves. I wondered whether it would help her to get through her exams, and it certainly did! I knew that it would bring calm to her during troubled times, but I didn't know whether it would be enough to get her through her exam and to help her physically sit in the room with all those people.

Unfortunately, schools do not seem to have time or the resources for children with anxiety. Sadly many children are saying that they have anxiety, and some of them really do not, but it is hard to tell which of them are just trying to pull the wool over the teacher's eyes, and which of them are indeed suffering as a result of this invisible mental illness. This makes me sad because those that are using this excuse to get out of class or to go home need to realise that they are making it harder for those who are genuinely suffering in silence.

Jess would come to me the day before the exam, and she would relax and feel calm. I would put on the music, and feel the energies gathering around the room. Jess is such a lovely girl and has such a sincere heart, but as I said earlier, in a crowded situation those with anxiety can be appear to be rude or ignorant. I have heard this so many times, and it makes me so incredibly sad. That person who is suffering is not ignoring you or being rude, they have social phobia, and it is a significant struggle for them in these situations. The next time you feel anyone is acting this way, please have a little compassion because the pain they are going through daily is beyond belief and is very real.

It is easy to socialise when you are a social butterfly like me and to chat to everybody whether you know them or not, but when you have anxiety it's as if you have trouble breathing and your heart is beating so fast that you just cannot bear to even say 'hello'. You smile and have that stare in your eyes as if the world is about to come to an end. This is a reality for these beautiful souls, and it is time the world took notice.

After her Reiki, Jess would find that she could sit through her exam without worrying too much and, yes, she did get through that day without having a panic attack, which was such a breakthrough for her. Jess would text me or phone me the day after and thank me so much for helping her. Many times, she turned up with a box of chocolates, God love her, which is her way of saying thank you, and they would be delivered with a big hug and a broad smile. But I have to say my waistline was getting thicker and thicker with each exam Jess took!

What a beautiful soul she is. I asked Jess to tell me her story and tell us how she felt during these sessions. Jess has found it challenging to put it into words, but I think you will agree this is a huge step for her to tell her side of the story. I offered to change her name, but she said no, because this book will help others who are struggling so much, and she wants to shout it from the rooftops, that coming here for Reiki has worked wonders.

Jess's mum wanted to let me know how she felt. Jess had hidden her anxiety well and seemed so good at home, that her mum had no idea what she was going through at school. She simply thought her daughter wasn't well. Few children tell their parents that they are going through anxiety, because, unlike other illnesses, it can't be seen. Many children and adults suffer anxiety and panic attacks in silence because they fear that nobody will believe them. Nobody else can see the pain that is going on within their bodies.

Clare- Jess's Mum

"I have no problems with Jess coming to see you for Reiki, I like that Jess is getting help."

Jess kept her anxiety to herself at the beginning, so I wasn't aware how much trouble she was having. I have tried to support her as best as I can, but it isn't easy if you are not picking this up in family life.

Jess was very reluctant to get any help from our doctor or other areas, so she didn't get any help at all. The thought of going to the doctor for help made her more anxious.

I am delighted with how you have helped Jess, and I am aware that she has become much more relaxed and confident within herself, and she is more independent now after receiving help from you. Thank you. x"

Jess's Account

Meeting people made me feel anxious and even people I knew made me feel this way because I wasn't that comfortable with them. Getting the bus or train was awful and I have been struggling for years. Going to school made me feel so stressed, making new friends has always been such a challenge I would feel sick in my stomach and wish I wasn't there. My anxiety makes me feel embarrassed and belittled. I felt like somebody was always standing over me, and the stress was controlling my life. At first, I didn't even know what it was I was going through; I just knew that it wasn't normal.

It hinders my life, that is for sure, as I wanted to do things other people were doing. My mum wanted me to get a job, and I just didn't have the confidence to go out and do that on my own, or even give somebody a CV for a Saturday job. It was awful, and I didn't understand why I was feeling that way. In school, I felt held back because I could not make friends as I had a sickly feeling in my tummy. It was tough to even get up in the morning and face the day at school. At the end of every year, the change from year to year and moving classes made me feel all tense and I didn't want to speak out about it.

As I believe Lynn has told you, I am her grandson's girlfriend, and so I knew Lynn well before I went for Reiki. But when I went for the Reiki for the first time, it also made me feel anxious in that environment. The whole family welcomed me into their lives, which made me feel at ease. I was shy at first, but they all make me feel a part of their family, which doesn't make my anxiety flare-up. I have been on many family holidays, which is lovely as Lynn and the others always treat me as if I am one of them. I really enjoy this time with them all, and I do think that being with them helps me a lot.

At first, I was scared and worried about having some Reiki. I worried about how it would make me feel and if this would make my anxiety any better, and I was frightened that it might make it worse. But going into Lynn's Reiki room was lovely. It felt calm and relaxed - it was quite strange really, and hard to explain. But even just walking through the doorway of the room suddenly settled my worries and anxiety. I know that is hard to believe, but I could feel the calmness come over me, it made me smile and sigh with relief. I felt a calm presence as I lay on the bed, and when the Reiki started, I began to feel like I was gently spinning, and I could see colours and feel a tingly sensation throughout my body. I love my treatment with Lynn, and it helped me so much. I take every chance I can to have a healing. It is so beautiful, and everyone should try it.

Lynn didn't just help me get through exams, but she also helped me with my life, and I feel like I can do more things now. I used to get anxious about getting the bus and train, but now I don't think like that, I feel more confident. I failed my GCSEs the first time around because the anxiety had taken over me. When I started going to Lynn, I could not face the exam room. So, Lynn started to give me healing the day before the exams, she also gave me breathing techniques to do if I felt the anxiety was coming on. This time, when going into the exam room, I didn't feel anxious. My belly didn't become tight, and my breathing didn't become heavy. I felt relaxed, and the night before exams, I felt fine too.

Lynn has very kindly given me a gift on this holiday. She has attuned me to my Reiki 1, which is the attunement for self-healing. This was an amazing experience, which I just cannot put into words. What an amazing gift she has given me. When I feel the slightest bit anxious, I now put my hands onto my stomach and send a wonderful energy into my tummy.

I cannot tell you the relief this has given me. I am seventeen years old with my life in front of me, and Lynn's treatments and kindness have helped me to move forward. She is such a lovely lady and always welcomes me with a smile and love. I know she has had many of her own challenges this year, with four bereavements that have affected her dearly, but she never turns me away, she opens the door with a smile and helps me to regain my confidence. I can pick up on people I don't feel are very nice, but being in the same room as Lynn is a great place to be. Thank you, xx.

"Helping one person might not change the whole world, but it might change the world for one person."

A Mother's Journey

This story has been told from both a mother's perspective and her child's own interpretation of how she felt. They were both brought to me by the Angels, I have no doubt of this. I would like to thank them both for stepping forward and being a part of this book. Many will undoubtedly benefit and find peace from their story, and so the story in their own words unfolds:

Debbie (mum)

When my Mum died, my seventeen-year-old daughter, Hannah, felt compelled to see a medium. This was something she did not really believe in before, so I was surprised she wanted to do it. I was happy to support this need because I had always been a very spiritual person even though I had never been to a medium before. I looked around to see where I could find a medium, and I was drawn to Lynn and kept coming back to her page whenever I did a search. I made an appointment as a birthday gift to my daughter, merely giving our first names to reassure that the meeting was totally open and providing no background information. I just hoped that my daughter would get some comfort from the session, but little did I realise what a significant impact that appointment would have.

My daughter had been suffering for several years with mental health issues and had experienced several traumatic events in her life. She had completely lost faith and hope in everything and could see no future. I had tried all the standard routes to get help for my daughter. Numerous medical appointments seemed cold and routine, treating the symptom but never really getting to deal with the underlying cause. I had literally tried everything I could think of and was desperate to bring her some respite and a glimmer of hope.

I accompanied my nervous daughter and prayed for a positive experience. The first thing we saw was a sign which had a significant connection to her gran, this sign was on the gate post of Lynn's home, so it provided some immediate reassurance. Lynn warmly welcomed us, and we began the session with an angel card reading. The first thing Lynn said was that the Angels told her my daughter had an issue with food, and that she needed to address this as she would need all her strength, and it was essential to look after her health to achieve what she was meant to do going forward.

This was a significant issue for my daughter, which no one knew about, but neither I nor any of the medical appointments had tackled this. Lynn then told my daughter that the Angels had said to her that "You don't know what this poor girl has been through." Lynn said my daughter had a gift for helping others, and would soon make a new circle of friends, where she would find like-minded people and that she saw a lot of books and studying ahead. We thought this was odd because my daughter's education had been disrupted due to personal events and she had left college with no plans to return. The amazing thing was that a few months later an opportunity arose, where she started a new course and indeed made new friends, who she connected with on a deeper level and who she could relate to, this then led to a job where she directly helped people in dementia care, this was amazing and is now back in college with plans to go to University. Lynn had explained there was a lot of healing needed for my daughter to move on with her life.

Lynn picked up that my daughter suffered from extreme anxiety which was affecting all aspects of her life. This was not something you would pick up if you met my daughter; it was something she had learnt to hide well. Lynn explained that as a mother, she had received spiritual help for her son when he suffered similar issues and had been paying this forward by helping other children directed to her. She believed that therefore we had found her, as her Guides had told her that they would send these children and their parents directly to her door. Lynn then offered some Reiki sessions and was confident she could help my daughter. I can't tell you how this made us feel. The relief, the hope, faith restored – finally, someone could see the pain and suffering and all she wanted to do was help.

At this moment, my prayers for my daughter were answered, Lynn was then able to connect with loved ones who had passed away. Her gran stepped forward, and Lynn accurately described how she had passed, and the detail was amazing. Consequently, this left us in no doubt as to whom this message was from. Lynn passed on messages of reassurance that Gran understood everything that was happening and that had happened around her passing. Lynn told my daughter how Gran loved and appreciated everything that Hannah had done for her, which was precisely what my daughter needed to hear. Gran also referenced a small black and white pet. Amazingly, we had recently got a puppy and my daughter had wanted to take her to see Gran, but she was too ill and then had died unexpectedly the very next day, so never got to meet the new puppy. It was great to know that Gran knew about this, which meant so much.

We left the session feeling lighter, with renewed hope for the future and with faith restored. My daughter felt so comforted that she was being watched over and supported from the other side. We returned for a Reiki session which really helped clear some emotional blockages and open the pathway and began the healing process. As a mother, you feel helpless watching your child suffer, lost and in such emotional pain. I was wracked with guilt and was feeling that I should be able to make it better. Lynn gave my daughter her Reiki sessions as a gift; she told us that this matter was so close to heart and that she knew it would help. I was elated and so thankful for meeting Lynn, it had proved to be a real turning point in all our lives.

Two years later, we felt it was time for another reading as we were moving into a new stage on our life's journey. Little did I know that this time my daughter wanted to return the gift to me and that the focus would be on what I needed. I should have guessed that Lynn and her all-knowing Angels already knew exactly what I needed, when the only appointment available happened to fall on my birthday! This made me smile, Lynn's gift was working before I had even arrived! I received some beautiful messages that gave me the strength and direction I needed to face some difficult decisions ahead. This would mean I could better support my daughter and leave behind pain from the past and positively move forward to a brighter future.

As expected, this session with Lynn was as beautiful as the first, and I thank Lynn for showing such kindness to both my daughter and me, and I don't doubt for one minute that many feel the same way. Lynn's gift is indeed a special one, she outshines many in her field, she is loving and kind, and nothing is ever too much trouble. It has been a pleasure to write our stories for this new book, and I hope that many mothers like myself who are struggling with their children, read this book and come forward to meet this kind and loving earth angel.

Hannah's Story

Anxiety had always been something I had struggled with since I was very young. I had quite severe anxiety leading me to have panic attacks often as a result of this. I struggle with OCD and PTSD, and anxiety is a mental illness that also goes hand in hand with them. In my experience, it is challenging suffering from any mental illness when you don't have an outlet as all the emotions turn inwards, and it becomes a cycle of repeated struggle.

I have always tried to find ways to combat my anxiety but usually ended up unsuccessful. These ranged from carrying a paper bag around with me when I was young, to avoiding social situations. My mum and dad struggled with me having anxiety, and it became extremely frustrating for them as they could see me struggling but didn't know how to help me. I had a lot of different 'triggers' that would make my anxiety worse such as busy shopping centres or talking about death, so I would do anything and everything to avoid situations and conversations I knew would make me anxious, which unfortunately made me feel quite isolated.

Keeping myself isolated obviously never created a resolution as I was just avoiding the problem rather than dealing with the issue. I then tried to attend counselling, and I went for a consultation, after which I was left feeling so humiliated and upset as I wasn't taken seriously, and they brushed off how much I was suffering. Even when I went to the doctor's, I was just offered medication, but I felt worse on it, and I didn't want to be on medication for months. It took me a year to come around to the idea to try counselling again, and I found another service and although psychologically I was provided with a lot of techniques to deal with anxiety such as grounding tools, emotionally I still really did struggle. I had tools on how to cope with panic attacks, but this didn't change the emotional hurt I felt that was causing the panic attacks in the first place.

I felt helpless, weak, and misunderstood. Anxiety is a very lonely mental illness, and it becomes incredibly frustrating. You feel like no one understands how you're feeling because you don't often understand it yourself and it becomes difficult for people around you, so it makes you feel very guilty to be affecting someone else. A significant role that perpetuates anxiety is trying to avoid and ignore how you feel in the hope that it will pass, as the more you don't deal with it, the worse it gets. It's easier said than done, however, as one of the hardest things to do is deal with the emotions you are feeling head-on.

There are so many emotions that make up someone's anxiety: Stress, fear, worry, depression, anger, nervousness and many more.

Anxiety always made me feel embarrassed and silly, and I'd still think, "Why can't I just get over it?" There are many 'symptoms', but as these can be both psychological and physiological, the overall effect of anxiety can be very intense and unpleasant.

Some examples of emotional symptoms were:

- Fearing something terrible was going to happen
- Worrying I was going to die• Worrying that my anxiety would lead to a panic attack
- Negative thoughts about myself, feeling I wasn't good enough.

Some examples of the physical symptoms were:
- Breathing difficulties
- Dizziness
- Restlessness
- Nausea
- Speaking extremely fast
- Dry mouth

It made me avoid situations and miss out on events I otherwise would have enjoyed. It isolated me at times from being around friends or family, but I'd feel so guilty about letting people down it would make my anxiety even worse. Anxiety always begins with a worrying thought, so for a long time, I would have these thoughts and just let them manifest before actively getting help and trying to deal with it. Anxiety often links with other mental health illness, depression and anxiety are found in many, but in my case with having OCD and PTSD, you often experience anxiety and a result of them.

However, there is a common link between all mental health illnesses, in that your emotions and thoughts are affected which then influences your actions and physical symptoms. People can't know what you're thinking or feeling, so a lot of people just observe the physical side effects and symptoms a person is experiencing and try to deal with them instead of the thoughts and emotions behind that. That's why I found with Reiki and connecting to the spirit world, from an emotional perspective, it is incredibly healing and resolving. The Reiki specifically made me feel I was emotionally and physically grounded and healed, and it was a powerful experience which makes it easier to have that mind and body connection and deal with the thoughts and emotions.

Going to see Lynn for the first time was a mixture of excitement, nervousness, and apprehension. My mum had always believed in spirits and healing, but I had still been somewhat closed off to the idea. Again, I link this back to the fear of death and the anxiety I felt around that. We initially wanted to see Lynn after my Gran had passed away as we wanted to connect with her, but I gained a lot more from our experience. When I went to see Lynn, I was at a point where I was desperate for help. My mum and I had tried so many different places for help, and we always felt like we were not being listened to or taken seriously.

It takes a lot to reach out and ask for help, and when you are turned away, it is incredibly disturbing. We got so frustrated and just felt like the world was against us. I didn't get any support from school, and we felt entirely alone. My mum was very worried as my mental health was getting worse and she didn't know how to help me. However, with Lynn we didn't even have to ask for help; she seemed to just know we needed it, she was very kind, welcoming and I felt entirely at ease, and for me, that was a miracle.

I can honestly say after seeing Lynn for the first time, it changed our lives. A lot happened before we saw Lynn that we believe lead us to her for help. I experienced a lot of trauma, especially in the last year. My dad tried to commit suicide several times, my uncle passed away, and then my gran also passed away the month after. For the first time, I was open to the idea of receiving healing, Reiki and connecting with spirits and felt like I was being drawn to visit Lynn, and I just kept saying to my mum, "I have to visit a medium." and then we stumbled upon Lynn online.

When we arrived at Lynn's house, we saw a lot of signs that made us feel we were in the right place at the right time. We were greeted with such warmth, and after the session, we were even offered a free Reiki session to help me with my anxiety, and this was the first time anyone had offered us help in this manner, as no one ever offered something for free before, and that act of kindness still means so much to me.

During this first session, it was also just reassuring to know that the people I loved so much were still around protecting me. Knowing they were okay helped me to cope with the grief and gave me hope that things would get better. Lynn mentioned to me things no one could even know about my past and in my life and just the acknowledgement that I had the spirits guiding me through such traumas, I never feel alone now.

I had my very first Reiki session and felt a calmness and a sense of content I had never felt before. I could feel Lynn's energy calmly sweeping through my body and mind. I went without panic attacks and anxiety for the first time in my life. A lot of opportunities opened after this, and I was a lot more willing to take them. It was an incredibly uplifting experience, and it was a pleasure meeting with Lynn and being introduced to her incredible work.

The main word I keep coming back to describe the experience is healing. I felt that I was being treated mentally, physically, and emotionally. I would strongly urge anyone struggling with a mental illness to see Lynn and have faith that there is help there. It helps you to genuinely heal right to your very core, I am convinced without a doubt that earth angels do exist, and I had been lucky enough to be drawn to one in my lifetime.

To close, Lynn had told us that she had been told many years before that this would be her destiny and that God's children who found themselves on the edge would be drawn to her for help. Thank You Lynn xxxx

James and His ADHD

I met James when he was just a teenager, seven years ago. He had lost his nan, who was his rock, his stability. She understood and always managed to bring James back down to earth after one of his episodes. His grandmother was the best in the world, I have been given to understand, though that is saying a great deal, to be sure. She was undoubtedly a perfect, kind old lady and she had silver curls and pink cheeks, as every grandmother should have. James spoke about her highly, and by reading the look on his face, he missed her dearly. Somehow, she just understood him. She never lost her temper with him; she would take a big long breath and distract him from whatever had kicked him off into one of his episodes. Her death had an adverse effect on James; it sent him into a frenzy of emotion, one that took a while to control. Unlike others, James found his grief never-ending, with a million questions buzzing around in his head, questions that just could not be answered, that was until he met me.

It was a beautiful summer's day, which was unusual for the UK. "Mostly cloudy with a spot of rain," the weatherman was more likely to say! I had a booking for a man, and the text message read, "I want a reading." That was a bit abrupt, I thought, but then

I felt a hand on my shoulder. "He needs us, Lynn," I heard in my head. So, I had booked him in and today was the day that I was to meet this abrupt man. There was a knock on the door, and, as my mum would say, it sounded like the bailiffs!! I jumped out of my skin and the dogs went mad, but I calmly composed myself and put on my best smile. There he stood, a mere boy, eighteen to be exact. As I opened the door, he just walked in, with no invitation. I smiled and closed the door.

"Hi, I am Lynn, and I am going to hope that you are James," I joked, pointing out the way to my workroom. James let out a loud laugh.

"I'm so sorry," he smiled. "Please don't think me rude."

"Not at all," I replied, showing him to his seat.

James was tall and dark with piercing blue eyes; he had a harassed look upon his face and scanned my room, taking in everything that was in there.

"Are you okay?" I asked, glancing over at his worried face.

"I don't know," he replied, anxiously.

"Please don't look so worried. You are okay in here and we will look after you." I calmly told him.

James had booked a reading. He said little as I laid out my Angel Cards. I could feel the anxiousness building inside this young man. One thing I did notice was that he had no guard up with me. This was fabulous, because it meant that he was ready to hear my messages and so it began. There were things about James's life that just flowed out of the reading. It was as if my Guides were painting a picture of James so that I knew who and what I was dealing with.

I felt quite nervous as I was picking up his energy. He was all over the place; it was like riding a rollercoaster! My stomach filled with even more butterflies of nervousness as we broached each step of his young life. I could feel my heartbeat, every single pound in my chest. This great pounding, this enormous pressure; every beat. I couldn't hear it, but I could feel it. It remains now, even as I write, and it persisted through what little of the self-control that I had left! I knew instantly that this was not mine, not my feelings, not my heartbeat. So, I paused for breath and reached out my hand, touching James on his arm and sending calm energy into his system.

"Please don't be anxious," I told him. "Everything will turn out, I promise."

I felt him relax and a sense of calm came over the room, thank goodness, as my head was in a spin and I was struggling to concentrate. Within an instant of James taking that deep breath and bringing calm to his body, I sensed a presence in my room. It was the energy of an older lady. The love she had brought

111

with her was terrific. She told me she was his nan, and I felt a great relief from her. She had been watching him from the spirit world and was saddened at his pain. The poor boy had been to hell and back, and now he was missing his grandmother so very much. She was so supportive of him in his life, but now that support had gone. He needed to hear these messages from her, he needed to know she was still there even if he couldn't see her.

The reading lasted around an hour, as James didn't want me to let his nan leave, which was understandable. It was after this rollercoaster of a reading that I asked James if there was anything, he wanted to ask me. James was with me for what seemed hours, going over his life, pain by pain and torture by torture. James told me that he sometimes heard voices inside his head, usually when he had *kicked off*, as he called it. These voices were calming and seemed to bring him back down to earth. Of course, I offered him Reiki, and yes, he wanted it right there and then.

"No time like the present, I suppose," I giggled.

The Reiki went well, and James said it was the calmest he had ever felt. This was a relief to us both. I was now exhausted! James was more relaxed when he left me, but before he left, he turned and gave me such a hug, with gratitude which came straight from that beautiful heart. James has continued with his treatments and his life, although still quite strange to some, has become more peaceful and more acceptable to those around him.

What is this label of ADHD? What is this illness that affects so many children and adults of today? I have come across so many different mental illnesses on my journey, and this is one of the most destructive., Are these just naughty children? Are they not being heard? I will give you some insight into what I have found over the years and let you make your own decision. James struggles to put things into words so he told me how he felt, and I wrote the following for him.

In James's Words

To be a child or an adult with ADHD is exhausting for most of us. We are forever stuck in that split second after explosion, both hurtling through space and static, on fire and frozen. Mine is the energy that seeks a thousand paths because the way forward is denied. I am the silent scream that's deafening, but you can hear it with your eyes if you dare look. I feel like a used car with a price sticker, only instead of numbers it just says ADHD, and no-one wants a problem car, do they? When I was tiny, I was taken to see a counsellor. The counsellor is lovely, she has toys, good ones. She laughs like she means it and answers my questions, even the ones that make other people angry. Then I'm back in class, back in the foster home, everyone's least favourite human. "James, finish your work," "James, sit down," "James, be quiet." For once, just for once, I'd love to hear "James, let's go race frogs, or James, let's jump on a trampoline, or Who cares about tidy bedrooms? Let's go build a fort in the woods." They never do, though. Never.

I carry a lot of medicine with me. I have an EpiPen because I turn into a splotchy red balloon when I get stung by a bee. I have an inhaler because I breathe worse than a bulldog on a treadmill. I have lactose intolerance, but I'm attracted to cheesecake like a moth is to a flame. The attraction is strong and equally as dangerous. Most of these are recent, but every school has said that since the second year I've carried medication in my system to alter my behaviour, to make me less agitated, less attention deficit.

The endless bounce in my feet and the rapid river of words tumbling from lips proved to be too much for those around me. The first pill my parents chose for me took my appetite until, at twenty-seven pounds too light they decided it just wasn't the right one. After that, I was given one that took my self-control until I was so impulsive, I would hide and run away for fun. After three years they finally decided, it just wasn't the right one. I've been on the same medication for nearly seven years now and have been attempting to get by with it less and less because, despite focus coming more easily, I can't stand the feeling of watching my body go through the motions of life without actually feeling anything. And though I can't stand the idea of taking yet another pill in the morning that makes me feel like somebody else, I do not attest the anti-depressants prescribed by my doctor. I know tablets are not a solution, nor a means to an end, but it is something to get me by till I find my way. Because problems cannot be fixed by pills, only the decisions we make when we're off them.

After talking with James, I realised that the lives of those living with ADHD are filled with structure and discipline, but this does not help. They are being drawn to Mother Earth, to be simple, not complicated, to love, not hate. Inside their bodies is an exciting explosion being held back, and you cannot contain an explosion very successfully, so what happens? A BIG BANG!

How sad this description makes me feel. There is no way out and even as a child you know that this explosion is coming, but there is no stopping it, so the energy wells up inside you and BANG! All is lost. It has happened and now all you can do is retrieve - your dignity.

After speaking with James, it became apparent that most people have a sort of mental secretary that takes 99% of irrelevant crap that crosses their mind and simply deletes it before we become consciously aware of it. It is like having a tiny computer inside your head taking stock of your thoughts and removing all that are useless, as such, the mental workspace is like a clean whiteboard, ready to hold and organise useful information.

People with ADHD do not have that luxury. Everything that comes in their mind gets thrown out there for all to see, no matter what it is, and no matter what common sense must be erased for it to fit. So, if we're in the middle of some particularly important task, and our eye should happen to light upon an object that catches our eye, for instance, a door handle, it's like someone burst into the room, covered in bright lights, heralded by trumpets, screaming HEY LOOK, EVERYONE, IT'S A DOOR HANDLE!

It may sound ridiculous to many of us, but this is life with ADHD, it's explosive and unpredictable. Why is it life takes souls from one uncomfortable place to another and allows them to shift between them? ADHD sufferers see an opportunity to choose to either be brave or move with the least of their fears like a leaf in a river. Sometimes they do flow like the leaf but are most proud of themselves when they just stop and take control.

There are days when their breath gets caught in their chest, and then they know the fear is gaining on them. Learning how to control their breathing and making it shallow helps them to find a way to release the tension. This isn't just present in children, it is also in adults, and can come across as severe aggression, although there are techniques that can help the symptoms subside.

The saddest part of all mental illness is that if the help is not there, then the patient becomes isolated and some of their lives are destined to end by their own hand. I genuinely believe that if we can just step forward and hold out a helping hand to all who need it, we can help to prevent this from ending so badly.

Angela

I met Angela some time ago, and as my Guides would tell me, "Nothing, my dear, is a coincidence." I always wonder how people who are so very lost in their lives happen to find me. Angela's story is like that.

We met in a restaurant and, to be honest, I didn't want to go out that night as I had been battling an annoying cough, which was quite the norm for me. Ray and I had gone out for our tea, which is a rare thing, as Ray also hates to go out because he suffers from PTSD. Ray doesn't like to go to crowded places like pubs or restaurants because those places make him feel very uncomfortable. Most of the time, we just don't go out, as the pain from his spinal injury causes him to suffer greatly.

However, on this rare occasion, we had gone out for our tea in West Kirby, which is relatively local to us. We had just sat down when I noticed a couple come in off the street looking for a table. The waiter asked if they had booked, but the lady just shook her head. Eventually, they were shown to a table, and the young woman sat with her back to the wall facing the room. I couldn't help but notice that she kept on scanning the room every time the door opened and looked very uneasy.

Our food had arrived, and Ray was already tucking in. *There is nothing wrong with his appetite*, I thought. The food was delicious. It was not long before we had finished, and as usual, Ray couldn't wait to get out of there. I had signalled to the waiter for the bill when suddenly the glasses from the young couple's table literally went up in the air! Everything on the table hit the floor in what seemed like slow motion.

I could see that the young lady was in rather a mess; her breathing was rapid. I had seen this many times before, and I recognised the symptoms from my own son. The poor guy that was with her looked like a rabbit caught in headlights, worried and panicking as he didn't know what to do.

Watching someone have a full-blown panic attack is not a pretty sight; it is frightening and very worrying. The person having the attack finds breathing difficult, their heart begins to race, they feel as if they are about to explode or at the worst, DIE!

This young lady, as I later found out, was called Angela. It was just before they had been brought their starters that Angela felt the dread building in her body. She felt the panic begin like a cluster of spark plugs in her stomach. The tension grew in her face and limbs, her mind replaying the last attack. Her breathing became more rapid, shallower.

119

In these moments before her personal hurricane, she understood the drug addict, or the alcoholic... anything to stop the primal surge to flee, to flee and not turn back, to escape from this place and from this feeling of torture.

The thoughts were accelerating inside her head. All she wanted was for them to slow so she could breathe but they wouldn't. Her breaths came in gasps, and she looked like she would black out. Her heart was hammering inside her chest like it belonged to a rabbit running for its life. The room was spinning, and she started to squat on the floor, trying to make everything slow to something her brain and body could cope with. She felt so sick and wanted to call an ambulance, but the thought of a hospital made everything worse. She was now on the floor in a ball- the foetal position. The panic had well and truly taken hold of her whole body. She had her hands cupped around her head, and the tears were dripping down her face. *This poor girl can't be much older than thirty*, I thought.

All of this happened in seconds. I put down my bag and moved over to where she was, which was now under the table. The boyfriend looked at me as if to say, *please help*, and luckily there was no one in the restaurant except for us four and the waiters. I knelt on the floor next to this poor girl.

"What's your name?" I asked. She didn't answer, but the young man said, "It's Angela. Her name is Angela."

I reached out my hand and touched Angela on her arm. "Angela, my name is Lynn," I said calmly. "You're okay. You're safe, you are having a panic attack. Take some nice controlled breaths for me then we can get you up off the floor lovely." As my hand touched her arm, I could feel the same energy as I had felt for many years coming from my own son. Angela took hold of my hand firmly and looked into my eyes.

"What was that?" she asked, climbing back onto her chair. I just smiled as I knew my Guides and the Angels had stepped forward. I sat beside her and told her to close her eyes, and to take some nice deep breaths in and hold, then let them out again. The whole time she was trying to control her breathing, I was calling in the Angels to come and help her. Angela began to take deep controlled breaths, and before she knew it, the panic attack had stopped. Her nerves were shattered, and all she wanted to do was go home. Her boyfriend grabbed their coats, and by the look on his face, he was happy to leave. Angela stood up and stared straight into my eyes.

"Thank you so much, I don't know how you did that, but you helped me more than you will ever know."

"Oh, I know, believe me, I know," I smiled.

Angela leaned forward and hugged me. I gave her a piece of paper with my number on it.

"I am being told that you are going to need this," I said as I placed it in her hand.

121

My heart was pounding by now, and I felt incredibly sad for the poor girl. It brought memories I would sooner forget, and they came flooding back to me. My Guides were right there, right beside me, helping me every step of the way, but I felt drained. The Angels' energy was explosive, and it had hit me head-on. I just wanted to go home now and put on my pyjamas. What a day! I had gone out for a quiet tea, and all hell had broken loose!

The weekend came and went, and I had a busy diary for the following week, Monday came and went and so did Tuesday. I absolutely love these days, as I hold my group meetings for spiritual development. I had gone to bed with a head full of Angels and beautiful messages from the spiritual teachers. Before I knew it, my alarm clock was going off, and it was time to get up. Is it morning I thought? I am sure I only just went to bed!

I looked at my phone which was sitting on my bedside table. The animals had heard my alarm go off and it was quite funny as I could hear them down the corridor licking bowls and playing tick with each other, cats and dogs running around like maniacs.

I was sitting having my cuppa when my phone went *ping*. I picked it up and noticed there was a WhatsApp message. I thought It would be my daughter saying good morning, but it wasn't, it was Angela, the lady I had met over the weekend in the restaurant. The message made my heart skip a beat, it just read, "PLEASE CAN YOU HELP ME?"

I messaged her straight back and asked if it was convenient to talk. The reply came back as a resounding YES. I called her straight away. I was hardly awake, and my first cup of tea hadn't kicked in yet, but I knew this was a definite call for help.

"Hi Angela, it's Lynn," I calmly said as she answered the phone. "What's up, lovely?" I asked her as there was a deafening silence on the other end of the phone.

"He has gone, and I don't know what to do," Angela began to cry uncontrollably. "He is the only real thing in my life, and he can't stand the upset anymore."

"Who has gone?" I asked her, cringing because I already knew the answer. I saw it in his eyes in that restaurant.

"Pete, my boyfriend," she replied, fighting back those floods of tears.

I looked at the clock; it was only 8am. I grabbed my diary looking to see what clients I had booked in for that day, but the diary was full to bursting. So was Tuesday and Wednesday. I felt a bit of panic as if I knew this lovely soul needed to be somewhere today. I asked Angela if she had anyone she could go and stay with, and the answer came back a very sad, no. I pointed her in the direction of her GP and all the usual places you would recommend. The phone fell silent again, then this quiet voice came back, "I just want to see you please," Angela politely replied.

I now was worried that I couldn't physically fit her in anywhere. I was working till 9.30 that night with my groups. What was I to do? I asked the Angels to help, and you guessed it my phone went *ping* again. I had received a text message from a client who had booked me for two hours, but the message read, "I am truly sorry Lynn, I was ok when I got up, but I had just started with the worst headache, so I am going back to bed, is it possible to rearrange our appointment, please? I am sorry it is short notice."

I smiled and replied, "Please don't worry, I will send you some dates. Now go back to bed and rest."

Of course, I had seen this many times before, and as the Angels had moved Heaven and Earth for Angela, it must be crucial that she has this appointment. She was so pleased when I told her I could see her at 10.30. I sent her my address and made myself another cuppa as the first one was stone cold.

I prepared my room, as always. I switched on the oil diffuser and put calming oils in it, I set light to my tea light candles in the glass tumblers which had beautiful sentiments written on them like, 'May your wishes have wings.' The room was almost ready, but I had one job left to do. I sat in my chair and prepared to call in the troops, the troops of Angels that is. I sat down and closed my eyes, and then I heard a giggle. I didn't have to call them at all, they were already there! The room filled with God's Angels, Angels of all shapes and sizes, the Archangels Michael and Raphael, the tiny Angels, the fairies, and of course, my beautiful Guides and teachers.

"WOW!" I said out loud. "What a presence!"

My Guides, Zach, and Clara, both stepped forward, and told me that the young soul who was coming here today had been guided to me. They told me how she needed a connection to her loved ones and connection to God. They said to me that she had lost her way and was on the edge and could not see any way out.

"You can help her Lynn; she needs reassurance that all is not lost."

I felt under quite a lot of pressure, but I was confident that the Angels and Guides could help this troubled soul.

10.30am came and right on time the doorbell rang. Angela stood there, looking pale and tired.

I welcomed her with a great big smile and showed her down to my room. Those of you who have visited me before know that when you enter my workspace, it feels like no other. There is an amazing sense of calm, that makes you want to kick off your shoes and curl up on the couch.

Angela walked down the corridor with her head slumped low. As I pushed open the workroom door, she raised her head and looked around the room.

"WOW!" she exclaimed, the look on her face said it all, the energy in that room had hit her as she walked in. "This is so lovely, it feels…" and she paused, "like Heaven," she continued letting out a huge sigh.

"Just a few of my friends," I smiled and asked her to take a seat.

Working with the Angels is an amazing thing to behold, and something I have learnt is that we must learn to listen, not give an opinion, or tell our stories, just listen. I only had to ask one question and the whole world of sadness opened before my eyes.

I watched as the Angels, both large and tiny surrounded Angela's whole body. She was sitting in a circle of light, and I knew she was safe; it was time for me to ask my question.

"Angela, tell me about yourself. Why have you come to me today?" I asked in a very gentle voice.

Angela raised her head stared straight at me and told her story from beginning to end. I stared at her and at times I was fighting back the tears, wondering how one person could go through so much in such a young life.

These painful memories, they're just the same as nightmares. Angela told me how she would take her painful memories and place them in a box; put them there with photographs, rings, and trinkets. But of course, they were still there even if they were locked away in that box. She told me of the voice in her head that kept on telling her that she was no good and that there was no point in being here, but there was another voice which told her that she was the one with the power to heal and be the person she was always destined to be.

As Angela told her story, I felt energies in the room change, and the Angels became a part of her, wrapping their energy around her like a warm blanket. I knew this sign; this was the sign that one of her loved ones was coming in to contact her.

As Angela's story unfolded, she never mentioned the beautiful soul that had just entered the room, I knew at that moment that the comment Angela kept repeating clearly was related to this female energy. She kept on repeating, "and then tragedy struck." I knew I would find out eventually what this meant, but I just wanted to let Angela get everything off her chest, because this was clearly something that she hadn't done before.

This beautiful soul beside me was Angela's mother. The tears were rolling down Angela's face by now as she just knew and could feel her mum's energy around us. It was all very moving, and the emotion was being controlled by the Angels and my

Guides, so that Angela would not be pushed over the edge again.

Her mother felt beautiful, and her energy was calming and serene, and I could feel the love between them. Your child always holds your soul in their heart, and your heart is forever theirs. Your child has your support always and they have your guidance should they ever wish to ask, both in life and in death. I would walk through the gates of Hell to keep my children and grandchildren safe and feel honoured to be given the chance, feeling only gratitude. Every child is a sacred gift, yours, and mine. We show our creator our gratitude by loving them with every power we possess, letting them explore, be adventurous, take risks... yet standing by to catch them if they fall. Let a mother's love, and a father's too, be the platform from which our children fly into clear blue skies, ever thankful to be such.

However, a mother's biggest dread is dying. We always feel that life will not go on without them. Who would hold us when we are sad? Who would dry our tears and make everything better?

Life does go on, but it's never the same. To lose a loved one is such a painful experience and it is something that leaves a lasting scar on your heart. I leant forward and, touching Angela on her arm, I told her, "Angela, I have your Mum here with us, are you okay for me to pass messages on?" Angela stared at me. "YES! YES!" she cried. "Please, tell me what she is saying."

Then something happened. I don't recall this ever happening before, but both Angela and I could hear a sound, a vibration, like a buzzing in our ears. I am clairsentient, so I don't usually hear anything. I feel all the emotion from the deceased, and it comes over me like waves of energy. Somehow, I just know who they are and what they want to say to me. But today was different. I could see my light catcher crystal gleaming around the room, which seemed very strange, as it wasn't the brightest of days. I heard a voice say, "She needs me now," then as I heard this voice, Angela looked up at me with a look of bewilderment on her face.

"Was that you?" she asked me with a look of shock.

"Was what me?"

"I heard you say, she needs me now," Angela replied.

The tears had suddenly stopped running down her face. I was in a bit of a daze as this had never happened to me before, and we both had heard the voice of her late mum.

I took Angela by the hand and told her that her mum was with us and that I had just heard as clear as day the same words.

The connection with her mum was an emotional one that day and It is something that will never leave me. I love my children and grandchildren

129

so very much but even for me, knowing that I can one day step forward and help each one of them gives me such peace.

This meeting with Angela was nearly three years ago now, and she has become a regular visitor to my workroom. Of course, we began Reiki healing straight away as this was what had brought her such peace in that restaurant that evening. The Reiki and many breathing techniques have helped Angela to cope with her anxiety; her healings were peaceful and rewarding for me. To be able to help someone like Angela has been an honour and a privilege.

What I hadn't told you in this story is the reason Angela had PTSD, but I am briefly going to do so now, with her permission.

Angela was part of a regiment in the Queen's Army. She had been deployed to Afghanistan and on her sixth tour, she was a part of the bomb disposal group that had been sent to search for land mines and hidden devices throughout the territory.

They had been busy all day, darkness was beginning to fall, and it was time to go back to base, when they came across a crashed car on the dusty road. Of course, they were suspicious of this as it was in the middle of nowhere, but it wasn't unusual to see cars littering the roads. Tatty and broken old cars were not kept in good working condition, so often broke down or were left abandoned at the roadside.

They parked their vehicle away from the crashed car and searched the area. There were four soldiers on that work party that day, two stayed with the vehicle and two set out to the car in question. Approaching the crashed car, they could see a woman covered with blood in the passenger seat, but no driver. They proceeded with caution, circling the car before they went towards it. Angela was one of the soldiers who approached that car, as she was also a paramedic. As they reached the car, which was on its side, they could see that there was no sign of the driver anywhere. They reached in to see if this woman was still alive, and Angela placed her hand on the woman's neck to feel for a pulse - this woman was not dead!

Angela turned around and headed back to the army vehicle for the first aid kit, but as she turned to walk back with the medical supplies, there was an almighty explosion. You see this car had been heading towards the army base when it had crashed, and the woman who was covered with blood was clearly the second person who was originally in the car. God only knows what had happened to the driver, but the woman had explosives strapped to her body, and she somehow detonated the device while Angela was heading back towards her. The soldier who waited with the woman was killed instantly; his body was unrecognisable. Angela was also severely injured but lived to tell the story. Both soldiers were given a medal, as this bomb had been heading towards the army base camp and was aimed at many soldiers.

Angela lost her dear friend that day; he had a wife and three children all under the age of twelve waiting at home in England.

Angela was sent home to recover from her injuries, and believe me, after spending time with this lady, the worst of her injuries could not be seen. Angela began therapies to help her to recover from the shock and horror of her friend being killed.

It was only twelve months after Angela came home that her mum was diagnosed with terminal cancer. She died six months later leaving Angela completely shattered. Could this girl take any more pain? There seemed to be nothing left in her life worth being here for. Angela underwent many years of psychiatric help, none of which even touched the sides.

The sound of that explosion still ringing in her ears, the sudden death of her mum, her rock, had completely pushed Angela over the edge. She had tried, what she called the coward's way out, suicide, and in her words, she couldn't even do that right. Angela just felt a failure, and on that night when she met me, she was about to lose her boyfriend too. Her world was in tatters and she had never experienced grief this bad before. Angela had lost her friend and colleague and her mum in one year. While writing this book I truly felt every emotion. I was also grieving for my mum and my best friend who had passed away within forty-eight hours of each other. This was an awfully hard time for me, and not everyone was sympathetic. That is hard to believe, isn't it? But people are sometimes so self-consumed that if they don't hear from you, they take it personally. They don't think that maybe, just maybe, you might need to hear from them. This had been true in both Angela's life and mine, and you realise who your true friends are when you are grieving so badly, and the people you need the most shut you out. I understood her plight and I felt her pain, and I feel that is why she could relate to me as a person.

Angela was in a place of desperation when we met with every memory playing like a song in her head, repeating itself for what seemed like forever. She was lost mostly because she had lost a big part of herself in her grief. She just couldn't get that part back and she wanted it so badly as she felt her life depended on it, but it was all gone, vanished into thin air. Angela described to me that at first, she thought grief was something bad that takes you ten feet under but soon she learned that it was just the price we must pay for loving someone.

It is something that we have no choice but to come to terms with, but when tragedy strikes twice, three times, four times, as it had with me in 2018, it is something that needs careful monitoring and an abundance of love from people around you. I was incredibly lucky that I am surrounded by my beautiful friends and family, some of whom I couldn't have got through the past twelve months without. Angela had no one; she was an only child, just her and Mum.

Angela's story is one of bravery and self-discipline, and although there are times, such anniversaries, that her grief comes back to haunt her. She is a long way down the road to recovery, both physically and mentally, and the most wonderful news is that she found the love of a man who understands her PTSD and supports her. Their life has taken an amazing turn for the better, and she is expecting her first baby any day soon. From this story comes a resounding sense of hope, hope that all who are suffering can find someone to reach out to, someone who will listen to them and show them love and respect, not push them aside as if they no longer matter. Compassion and love are qualities only few have, and most people only see themselves and their problems. The Angels put Angela and me together and saved her life. Reiki healing has been a godsend to Angela, and I thank God every day that I was there in the right place at the right time.

My spiritual team have taught me to find gratitude in my life and when In darkness, Believe in light, In loneliness, Believe you have friends,
In sorrow, Believe you have joy,
In pain, Believe there is empathy,
In frustration, Believe in patience,
In anger, Believe in perspective,
In indifference, Believe in love,
When we are subjected to negative believe that some positive will come out of every situation and this will bring hope for us all.

Christopher

This is the hardest part of my book to write. My youngest son had difficulties from the very first day he drew breath. He had the most traumatic of births; he was born with the umbilical cord around his neck. This was terrifying as it was wrapped around many times; he was born after many hours of labour, but he had been almost strangled by his cord. The birth was horrific, and I think that they realised he should have been born by a caesarean. But it was all too late as by the time the hospital realised what had happened, he was already in the birth canal and was suffocating. He was literally dragged from my body, and the resuscitation team were on standby.

They managed to bring him around and told me all was okay. He had a few bruises on his body due to the trauma and what looked like rope marks around his neck, but it would all clear up and he was a strong, healthy boy. You may be wondering why I am telling you this story; it will all become clear and show how a miracle was given to a desperate mother and how it had an impact on twenty-six years of a young person's life.

The truth is, he was far from okay. My poor boy always looked so sad, and from an incredibly young age, he wouldn't speak to anyone and struggled with socialising. Even as a one-year-old, he would panic at the thought of going anywhere he didn't know. Even a trip to the shops or to a family get together proved terrifying for him. He didn't sleep for longer than a couple of hours at a time, which was exhausting for everyone in the household, as he would scream as if he was terrified.

I had taken him to the doctors more times than I care to mention; when I look back, it was all so very frightening. The doctors concluded for the next four years of his young life that he was just a naughty child! I think that was their way of saying, *we don't know what's wrong with him!*

Both his father and I were at our wit's end; we just didn't know what to do. You should have seen my son – he was so beautiful, with the face of an angel, he had white-blond hair and the darkest brown eyes. He was such a handsome little boy, but his soul was so troubled. I would hold him tight and tell him, "It will be okay, Chris, I promise. If I could take this away from you, I would but I don't know how."

He didn't have many friends growing up, but there was one specific family who lived in the house opposite ours where he would make a special bond. Their young boy, Michael, was the same age as Chris, and they got on very well. Chris didn't seem to mind going to their house and playing when he was young; they grew up together and both started school at the same time. Tracy, Michael's mum, was on his list of trusted adults.

My best friend Helen also had a son who was two years younger than Chris, and because I saw so much of Helen, Chris and Mike became friends. Helen was very intuitive. She was such a good person to have around you, and we complimented each other perfectly. We have been the best of friends for over forty years now and we will continue beyond into the next chapter of our lives and once our life here has finished.

Christopher's school years were a disaster. He couldn't endure school; the anxiety was building and building inside my little boy. Somehow, he managed his way through his first school, but towards his eighth birthday, things seemed to be getting worse. The classes were too big, and it was all just too much for him. Without a doubt, his education was suffering.

It was at this time that we decided that it would be a good idea to look for a smaller school, or private education. We found a school in Hoylake, on the Wirral, and Chris began the happiest of his school years there. He made friends with a boy called Jim, who came from a lovely family who lived close by. Jim became another of Christopher's lifelong friends, and his family have always treated Chris as if he were one of their own. Nothing was ever too much trouble and in my lovely friend Carol (Jim's mum), I have much to be grateful for.

I don't know how Chris managed to get through to his sixteenth year, but finally, that year came and with it the stress of his final exams. As you can imagine, he didn't do very well at all, but God love him he decided that he would continue his education and go to Sixth Form College. He seemed to be happy at the College and it was less formal than his school years. He started to flourish and enjoyed the College very much. He met a nice girl there who seemed to match Chris completely. She wasn't pushy and realised that Chris didn't want to do all the things the other lads were doing, like partying till morning, drinking or smoking. He just wasn't interested.

Then tragedy struck. Christopher's dad and I had separated a couple of years before. I always loved Ken from the bottom of my heart, but he had his own issues; he had come from a difficult childhood, his mum was abused by his dad, who was a heavy drinker. He came from a big family: five boys and five girls. The boys seemed to inherit the father's drink problems, but thankfully that was all that Ken inherited. He was a kind and loving man and he loved me with every breath in his body, but the drink was a problem. I always heard a voice saying *he must stop, he must stop*. His own father died at quite a young age from cancer of the stomach due to excess drinking through his life. I begged my husband to stop drinking but he couldn't, and I know now that drink was his hiding place, as he too couldn't cope with people.

Christopher never lost touch with his dad, although the break-up was very painful for all involved. I thought that if I gave Ken the ultimatum to stop drinking or we wouldn't last, that he would stop. But that never happened. It was incredibly sad; hearts were broken when we split.

Things went from bad to worse and our break-up had gone too far, so we never got the chance to reconcile the marriage. I think we were both as stubborn as each other. I do know that neither of us wanted this, to split up a family is not an easy decision. But we eventually divorced and sadly all was lost.

I met my husband Ray about three years after Ken and I split. I know it's hard for a child as no man can replace their father, but Ray is a kind man and has always treated me well and we have been married now for ten years.

It was one cold November morning and there was a knock at the door. I was sitting in the living room at the back of our little bungalow and Ray went to answer the door. As Ray walked up the hallway, that voice in my head told me to take a deep breath. I felt a panic come over me; I didn't even know who was at the door, but I knew something was terribly wrong. I heard a familiar voice; it was a friend of mine and Ken's. As soon as I heard her voice, I jumped up. I ran into the hallway where she stood looking at me.

"Lynn, something terrible has happened."
I burst into tears. "Where is he?" I said. "What has happened to him?" Without her saying his name, I knew she had come to tell me something about Ken. What came out from her lips next will stick with me for eternity.

"I am so sorry, Lynn; Kenny was found dead three days ago!"
I just broke down. "No!" I cried. "My boy! What will I tell him?"

I lost control and was distraught.

"This will kill him – what happened?" I asked. She continued to tell me that he had been ill and told no one; he walked out from hospital, went home, and died in his bed. He had been diagnosed with stomach cancer, but it was all too late. It had taken over his body and there was nothing the hospital could do for him.

I was devastated and I just didn't know how I was going to break this news to Chris. The anxiety in him was already very prominent, this would just be so distressing to him.

Chris had already gone to College. I phoned and told them what had happened and that I would be sending his stepfather to bring him home. How do you tell any child one of their parents has tragically died? My heart was racing as I heard the front door open. Chris and Ray walked in and I don't remember a worse moment ever, than when I had to tell my son that his father was gone. He took the news very quietly, stood up and went to his room.

The next days passed quickly, but Chris, as one might predict, was growing increasingly quiet. We pushed through these weeks tenderly, and with the funeral over, he went back to College. He was surprisingly calm, but my voices were telling me different, and to be aware there was something happening in the quiet of Christopher's mind. I kept a close eye on him, making sure not to smother him. Then the terrible day came I had a call from College to tell me no one could find Chris. He had signed into College in the morning but hadn't turned up to class.

The teachers were aware of what had happened and that he suffered with severe anxiety, so alarm bells rang when he was missing from class. I called and called Christopher's mobile phone, but he wasn't answering. I was worried sick…where could he be? I got in my car and went looking for him. Where would he go? My mind was chaos and I couldn't think straight. Because of his anxiety, he couldn't use buses or most public transport, so I figured he would be heading home on foot.

I couldn't find him anywhere but then he

answered a text. "Come and get me, Mum." That's all it said. I found him on the main road heading home. He wouldn't speak when I picked him up, he just said," Take me home please," and nothing more. I called the College and told them he had been found. This was just towards the end of the year. He had taken his exams for that year and had A+ with distinction. I was so immensely proud of all his hard work. But that day he walked out from College would be the last time he would ever return.

Christopher's anxiety had taken over his mind and body. His father's tragic death had pushed our son over the edge, and the years that were to follow would forever stick in my mind.

On that day in 2010, my lovely son took to his room and didn't come out again for three years! His anxiety had consumed him completely. We tried everything to bring him back into the real world, but nothing could convince him that there was anything out there that was worth his time. He didn't see friends or family; he had isolated himself from everyone except me and my mum. His bond with his nan was unbreakable. She loved him so much that every time she visited, he would break the mould and come downstairs to see her. The doctors told me Chris was grieving and I was to let him do so in his own way, but anxiety and grief was not a good combination. Chris lived in the dark. He had lost a lot of weight through his illness and things just escalated.

I had been having some terrible financial problems, because, during the property crash of 2007/8, I had lost a lifetime's work and all my savings and income from twenty years of hard work. This had left us in financial ruin, but my Guides and Angels were telling me to go get it, this house is for you and you must move quickly.

The house they were talking about was a farm called Greenacres this farm was located down old Lingham lane on the Wirral. As a child I would walk past this house with my family and dream of how I would live there one day. How I loved this little farm, everyone would laugh at my daydreaming, but in my head, I was being told that one day I would live here in this special place.

As a child I just knew this was true, but as an adult I always wondered how I would make this possible. But you see the spirit world with circumstances and a strange twist of events had delivered to me what was promised some 40 years earlier.

To say Heaven and Earth were moved for us to move here is an understatement! I was told it was here that Chris would recover." Do everything in your power, Lynn, this house is meant for you." I thought my voices were absolutely nuts! How could I afford this house? Where was the money coming from to pay a rent that was so far out of my reach?

So many questions – I felt as if my head would explode! Spirits guided me every step of the way, although at this time in my life, I still wasn't aware of whom it was that I could hear in this head of mine. But nevertheless, I went ahead and took a massive step and went after that bungalow with what felt like the force of the heavens behind me. "You have work to do there," I heard a voice say. "Now move yourself. You have no time to waste."

I found a tenant for my little bungalow, and we moved out of there and into the farm in November 2011.

When we moved, Chris was excited as the farm was to give him so much freedom. The bungalow was set in five acres of land, right on the seafront. Chris would heal here, I was told by spirits, "but it will take time. Just trust in what we tell you."

The first twelve months were difficult; there were a lot of repairs to do, and things were difficult with money. However, we struggled through and made it work. I was happy to have my beautiful horse outside my window again. *This is the life* I thought; *things have got to get better here*. We were sent here for a reason, and now I had to find out what that reason was.

Things didn't quite go as I thought. Chris went from bad to worse and in our lovely new home his life became darker, and his anxiety seemed to have consumed him. Over the next couple of years, Christopher's anxiety got so bad he stopped coming out of his room at all until we were in bed or out of the house. I had spoken to doctors about him and they tried to get through to him but to no avail. I was worried for his life; he had lost about three stone in weight, his skin was pale, and his body was weak. He had given up on life, and at the age of eighteen, he told me he was finished.

"I am no good, Mum. Who would want me? I can't breathe when others are around. What is the use?" he would ask me, "What is the use?"

To hear these words coming from the mouth of your child is the most painful experience ever. I would hold him tight and try to reassure him. My own stress levels were through the roof; my blood pressure was terrible, and nothing seemed to stabilise it. As Chris got worse, my heart was breaking in two.

I felt so alone. Although I had family around me, my sisters and my brother had their own lives to think about, so Christopher's troubles were not foremost in their minds. I know this wasn't intentional, but I really don't think they ever understood the devastating torment that both Chris and I were going through and sometimes it felt as if we were going through it alone.

It was then I started to ask my father who had died many years ago for help and I begged Ken,

Christopher's dad, to help our boy. "I don't know what to do," I would cry. "I am going to lose him. Please, someone, help us!" The desperation had taken over me now, and I felt bad things happening.

The last straw was the day Chris locked himself in his bedroom and barricaded the door. His cousin Tania, whom he loved like a sister, was here with the horses. I shouted to her to come and help me to speak to Chris. He told us both to go away. He never let me into his room, he kept it dark, and I would leave his food at the door.

This was a desperate situation. I had tried to get in, but he would not open the door.

"Please, Mum, just go away, leave me alone."

I felt something bad would happen this day if I just walked away. I threw myself at the door breaking the lock and Tania, and I pushed the door open. He was upset at what I had just done but I was so glad we had done this as I think he had given up that day. I don't want to think what would have happened if I had just walked away.

I heard a voice telling me it would be okay – *he has a friend around the corner*. As you can imagine, I had no time for these voices; I thought I was going mad!

I made a phone call to the doctor; our usual doctor wasn't there, so I asked for any doctor to come visit him as I thought that he was now in a desperate state of mind.

It was around three hours later when I heard a knock at the door. A young Indian man stood on the doorstep; I opened the door and he stepped inside. I asked him into the living room, and we spoke for a while about Chris.

"I cannot believe what I am hearing!" he said. "Why has this become so bad?"

I explained that Chris took to his room after losing his father and hadn't been in public since. The doctor was shocked, to say the least.

"I cannot allow this," he said with a sharp tone to his voice. "Please fetch him to me."

I explained that he hadn't seen anyone but me for three years and that it might take me a while to coax him out. I went to Christopher's door, which was locked from the inside.

"The doctor is here, please come out," I said.

"No, Mum, I can't," said Chris. "Please, Mum, ask him to leave."

"No," I said, "come out, or I am coming in!"

I heard a click and the door unlocked. Chris came out and very sheepishly entered the living room.

The doctor looked shocked.

"I cannot believe my eyes," he said. "You look so weak and terrified at the very thought of speaking to me." Then he stuck out his hand. "My name is Dr J and I am here to help you, Chris. Your mum has told me everything and I cannot allow this to happen to such a young life."

Chris shook the hand of the doctor, and a smile came over his face. After a good chat, the doctor decided that medication was the way forward just to stabilise him. Chris shook his head, "I don't want tablets."

"These will help," the doctor said, "just give them a try. I will come back and see you in five days."

Chris agreed, and the doctor left while Chris went back to his room.

I heard a familiar voice say, "Don't worry Lynn, don't worry." I still didn't know quite who these voices were, I just knew they would help me as they have always done in my life.

I thought we had made a breakthrough. I felt confident that this was the way out of his terrible situation. The doctor came back after the five days and made a pact with Chris.

"I will see you every week," he told Chris. "Is that okay?"

"Yes," Chris replied with a smile.

"However, this is the last time I will come and see you at home."

Christopher's face dropped. "What do you mean?" he asked the doctor.

"You will come to me at the doctor's surgery."

I could see the terror in Chris's face.

"You will come every Monday when surgery is over. I will see you and pick up on your progress every week."

Chris reluctantly agreed, however, the first time he was meant to go, I just couldn't get him to walk out of the front door. You see, he hadn't been out of the house in years and the thought of it sent him into a panic. The doctor yet again came to us.

"This is the last time Chris, I am a terribly busy man, do you understand?" he said." Please, you must try and come to me."

The next Monday came, and Chris managed to get into the car and go to the doctors. I felt as if Heaven and Earth had moved for him that day. He had made the first step outside of the house. I knew this was not going to be a quick fix, but it was the first step of many.

During these times, I asked for help from God and the Angels every night.
"Please help my son," I would beg. I would feel comfort in knowing my dad and Christopher's dad would be listening, but frustration in the fact that I couldn't speak with them.

During one of his many trips to the doctors, I was called in the room with Chris to discuss the next step. The doctor told me that Chris hadn't had closure on his father's sudden passing, and he said it was time to spread his father's ashes and put him to rest.

I did not have Ken's ashes – his brother had them. I had asked him not to spread the ashes before contacting me first, as this was Christopher's dad, and I felt he should be present when this was done. I called his uncle and asked if we could have the ashes, as Chris needed closure. To my surprise, he told me, "I am sorry, but I have done it already." I was shocked and upset at this as he had promised that he wouldn't do it without us. On reflection, I realise it must have been hard for him too, this was his brother and they were close, and it was now over three years since his death.

I had the awful task of having to inform Chris what had happened. He quietly stared at me and said it was okay, but I could see on his face that it was far from it. The only consolation was that Ken's brother had told me that the ashes had been spread where they had all spent many holidays, fishing from the rocks on Anglesey.

This made Chris smile when I told him, as this was his dad's favourite place in the world. I told him that we could go and visit and say our goodbyes to his dad one day and Chris agreed but time went on and still the only time Chris left the house was to go to the doctors. He never ventured out anywhere else, even with me in the car. He was still in that bad place where desperation could take over him quickly. I continually tried to get him to come out with me, anywhere, it didn't matter, I just continued to ask him, and the answer was always, "NO!"

It was a July morning, midweek if I remember rightly. I was awoken by the feeling of desperation. I cannot explain how that felt, only to say that I jumped out of bed, thinking something was wrong with Chris. I flew up the corridor and to Christopher's room. I tapped on the door but there was no answer, so I opened the door with the excuse I was letting the cat out. Our big tom cat, Tiger, always slept with Chris from the minute we got him but always knocked on the door in the morning for me to let him outside.

On opening the door, I realised both the cat and Chris were fast asleep, so I went and made myself a cup of tea and pondered on what on earth had woke me up. A friend was staying with us at the time in our spare room as she had broken up with her husband and was in between homes. As if I didn't have enough on my plate here, I had said she could come and stay a while until she sorted herself out. I told her of this awakening that I had experienced that morning and that it felt so real. As I was telling her, I could hear something or someone talking to me as clear as day.

"Get him out!" this voice was saying. "Get him out!" Then it all came to my mind as if someone had opened the floodgates to Heaven and they were shouting to me: "GET HIM OUT!" I was shocked by this, as although I have heard voices all my life, this

151

was different. This was clear and precise. I looked at my friend and knew straight away what I must do.

"We have to go to Anglesey," I told her. "We have to go today."

She looked at me, astonished.

"Oh my God," she said. "We can't, he will be ill – he will have a panic attack!"

It was early in the morning and early morning was never a good time for Chris. I decided I would wait until around eleven and wake him up then and tell him what we were going to do today. I could hear a voice saying, *it will be okay, Chris will come, he will be fine*. I felt sick to the bottom of my stomach! I woke Chris and let him properly come around before I told him of my plans.

I felt confident that what I was hearing was all going to go very smoothly and to plan. What they didn't inform me of was the reaction I was about to receive from my son. He completely went into meltdown; he had a panic attack at the thought of jumping in my car and driving all that way. I was upset and Chris was in a right state!

Well, that didn't go as I thought it would, but there were no voices; all were silent.

I felt very much deflated, all that upset, and I still hadn't got him out of the house. I spoke to him later that day; I told him I was sorry about the upset, but this was something we would need to do, to move on in life. Chris being Chris, he was so understanding. He knew exactly what I was trying to do and knew how much he was loved and that I only wanted what was best for him.

I went to bed that night feeling very emotional. I had watched my son all his life goes through turmoil after turmoil. I was worn out, both emotionally and physically. I must tell you; my prayers were strong that night! I wanted to know why this was happening to my beautiful son, why God had forsaken this boy who had such a big heart and a beautiful soul.

The rest of the week went by quickly. I went to bed on Friday night feeling quite calm really, and Chris had been sitting outside that afternoon with my friend and me in the gorgeous summer sunshine. He looked happy and carefree sitting there laughing with us. But of course, he was within the boundaries he had set for himself; he was in the safe zone.

It was around 4am on Saturday and I awoke with the same feeling I had experienced on that Tuesday morning. I sat up in bed feeling quite emotional, but this time I felt strong as if someone had lifted me up and given me an injection of strength. I got up out of bed and went to the kitchen to make some tea. It was a lovely morning and I opened the patio doors and watched the sun coming up over our beautiful home. It was surprisingly warm for that time of the day.

The birds were singing, and for a moment, I felt I didn't have a care in the world. A complete feeling of peace surrounded me and then it happened, the voice came back. *It is today*, it said. *Prepare yourself,* and then as you might imagine, that feeling of peace turned into dread. Suddenly, I felt a force surround me. It was now around 7am and I felt a strength that I knew, a strength that I recognised. I felt a love and strength from my father and my ex-husband that is difficult to put into words. I felt their collective energies merge with mine, the power and determination welled up inside me. The spirit of my loved ones was pushing me forward. I showered, got dressed, opened the gates to the farm, filled the car with what we would need for our journey and I was ready to go.

My friend, who was quite an emotional woman, found herself in a real state of distress.

"You can't do this, Lynn," she kept saying. "He will be ill; he will be upset."

The voice in my head told me to tell her to be quiet; we were going, and I didn't want to hear any negative emotions about it. She looked at me, crying.

"Either you're with me or not," I told her, "but either way, my son is going to Anglesey today."

She pulled herself together and went to her bedroom to get her camera and prepare for our journey.

There was no sadness or fear in my body. I

felt positive and driven. It was now 10 am; the car was ready, and so was I. I walked into Christopher's room and announced to him that he was to get up, as today we would go to Anglesey. He took one look at me and put his head under his covers. "Don't Mum," he said. "I feel sick."

The voice of his father was in my ear. *Move him*, he was saying. *Today is the start of the rest of his life.*

I felt a strength come from my boots! I pulled the cover away from him and told Chris to get up. He started to panic, and then the voice within me shouted out as if I was possessed by my late husband.

"Get up!" I shouted. "I don't care if you feel sick, we are going! Now get your bucket and your water and get in the car!"

I felt the strength of a thousand horses running through my body! Chris got out of bed.

"I can't Mum," he said. "Please."

Usually, I would weaken as this was my son; my heart would be wrenched out of my chest watching him suffer this way. But not today. I was not myself, that's for sure. I was standing there as two people, myself, and my late husband. I felt his strength beside me, and he wasn't taking no for an answer.

Chris surprisingly grabbed his sunglasses and his headphones and got into the car.

My friend stood there in amazement. She pleaded with me to stop, not to do this.

"Get in or get out of the way," I told her sternly. She climbed into the back seat of my car and I started the engine; my heart was beating out of my chest. I had done it; we were on the way.

The Journey to Freedom

That one-hundred-mile journey was the quietest time I have ever spent in a car. Chris didn't even look at me and he was angry with me. He listened to his music and looked straight ahead. The familiar journey, which I had made so many times in my lifetime, went very quickly. We arrived on Anglesey to bright blue skies and warm sunshine. I felt a calm come over me; I had done it! What a feeling that was and we were a hundred miles from the door that Christopher had been prisoner behind for many years.

I always get a feeling of love, a feeling of home, as I cross the Menai Bridge to our special island. Today was no different, I was home, and my son was with me.

We headed along the road to Llygwy Beach, the place we had spent so many happy years with Chris and his father. We arrived at a very packed car park, and in the summer months, there is always a parking attendant on the entrance. As we passed the entrance, Chris spoke up for the first time in two hours.

"There's Alan," he said.

I looked at Chris and asked, "Where?"

"There," he replied, pointing to a man on foot just leaving the car park. I looked at Chris lovingly and told him that it wasn't his uncle, he was just wishing it was because it felt familiar to him.

"I know my uncle," he snapped at me. My friend told me to run after him and see if it was while she went and bought a parking ticket.

I thought I would humour Chris and started out of the car park on foot after this man; I caught up with him and tapped him on the shoulder and to my surprise when he turned around, I realised it was indeed my son's uncle! What a surprise! I couldn't believe my eyes.

"Oh, my God!" I said to him. "What are you doing here? I have just arrived, and I have Chris with me; it's the first time he has been out of the house in years!"

Chris's uncle just stared at me in amazement.

"Do you still come fishing here?" I asked.

"No," he replied. "This is the first time I have been in three years; the last time I came it was to spread Ken's ashes.".

"I can't believe you are here the same day as us!" Then to my surprise, he told me how he was awoken with a shock at four o'clock that morning. "I knew I had to come," he told me, "but I didn't know why."

He showed us where the ashes had been scattered and then my friend and I went for a walk and left Chris and his uncle to have a talk and reminisce about the good old days and their fishing trips with his dad. As I walked away, I saw my son's face in a different light. He was laughing and was so happy to be there in that beautiful place.

On my return, Chris told me that he wanted to go to the place where he sat for so many hours with his father. This was on the cliffs between Llygwy Beach and Moelfre, the fishing town. Chris, my friend, and I set out across the cliff walk towards the overhanging cliffs that he knew so well.

My friend was a budding photographer, and she had brought along her camera. It was quite a walk to where Chris wanted to be, so he ended up ahead of us while we oldies dragged behind. My friend's camera had a powerful lens. She stopped along the walk to take pictures of all sorts of things. As we turned a corner, she called me back.

"Look," she said, "look at Chris – what is he doing?"

I looked through the camera and there he was, sitting on the platform where he and his dad had spent so many happy hours together. He couldn't see us, but we could see him through the lens.

He had a huge smile on his face and looked as if he was talking with someone; he was happy. I felt all sorts of emotions welling up inside of my heart. He was free, and like a caged bird, the spirit of his loving father and grandfather had set my son free.

As we caught up with Chris, he stood up and hugged me. We were both feeling very emotional.

"I love you, Mum," he said, "and I couldn't have done this without you." The tears rolled down my face in complete happiness.

It was time to move from the rocks and go for a drink. It was mid-afternoon now, and the sunshine was beating down on us. We had started the walk back to the car park when Chris decided we should scramble down the rocks and walk back along the beautiful Llygwy Beach. My friend and I giggled.

"How the heck are we getting down there?" she said. "We are going to break our necks." We both laughed and held hands to guide each other down.

Chris was ahead of us now and was in the distance walking along the beach and then suddenly, my friend said to me, "Who is that with Chris?" I could see a man and a woman but couldn't make them out clearly. Then he started hugging them." What on earth is going on?" I wondered. Chris didn't hug anyone but his nan and me.

What happened next was amazing! I reached the spot where Chris was standing, and I was so shocked to see my old friend and her husband. Tracy was Michael's mum and Michael is the young boy who Chris was particularly good friends with most of his life.

"Oh, my God," I said out loud. "What are you two doing here?" We hadn't seen Tracy for many years.

"We are staying on the other side of the island," she told me.

"We went to the paper shop this morning, and there was an elderly lady who told us that the sunshine would be lovely on this beach today. So, we got in the car and drove over, and we have been here all day."

Christopher was overjoyed; his uncle and old friends all gathered on his favourite beach. We said our goodbyes and drove to the opposite side of the island to Rhosneigr. I couldn't visit our island without going to say hi to my dad, whose ashes were laid to rest in his favourite place not far from the airfield at RAF Valley.

My son looked at me with such a loving glance.

"Thanks, Mum," he said, "for organising all of that."

"All of what," I asked?

"For getting everyone in one place for me today, important people who meant such a lot in my life."

"I didn't do anything," I told him. He looked at me and smiled then, as we pulled up in the car park of Ty Hen, I saw the most amazing thing. For a split second, I saw my lovely dad and my deceased husband standing on the hill.

My heart filled with love and emotion. None of this was a coincidence; Christopher's father and his beloved grandfather had indeed moved Heaven and Earth that special day, to bring us all together in one place.

We had been guided by spirit, all of us. The 4am wake up call for me and Christopher's uncle, the old lady in the paper shop bringing Tracy over to the other side of the island; all of this had been orchestrated by the spirit of our loved ones. On hearing my plea for help, they delivered in a way that usually only happens in the movies.

My son had been delivered back to me, and this day was to be a true awakening for both of us.

Christopher's story continues to grow, as does his strength. The drive home was not as quiet as the drive there; it was filled with light and love. Chris was not out of the woods yet, but by God's hand, was certainly pointed in the right direction.

It was this awakening that had a profound effect on both my son and me; there was no turning back now the spirits had found their way in and my life would never be the same again.

There are many reasons I have shared my son's story in this book. It is so personal to me, but I know there are many parents out there who are battling against anxiety within their child, and I wanted you to know that you are not alone. Life is exhausting when you have anyone around you who suffers with mental illness, but there is always hope for you and for them. My son still suffers with anxiety and struggles immensely with social anxiety.

But with the help of Reiki healing and the intervention of my spirit family my son gained his life back for three whole years! He passed his driving test, first time, he began to go to the gym, and I thought life was beginning for my lovely son. I was however wrong. Unfortunately, my mum passed away last year, and this has sent Chris's anxiety spiralling out of control again. He is back in his room, all 6ft2 of him and this time I don't seem to be able to shift him.

He does not deal with grief very well, but he will find his way again and learn to live with the loss. But in the meantime, he is stuck. I am working on his Reiki treatments, and I have now studied my Karuna Reiki, which I have done for Chris, and my grandchildren. I will not let anxiety take over our lives again; it will not beat us down. I will continue to help my son, as much as I possibly can. I know that healing will ease his mind and perhaps give him back a life.

With any mental illness, it is a case of don't give up, even in the face of adversity because we *can* make a difference. I know that Christopher's story has inspired many to seek help. The stories within the pages of this book are stories of hope, and if reading this helps just one person, then I have achieved what I have been asked by the Angels to do.

Unbreakable Bond

In my book, A Light to Guide Us Home, I told a story of my goddaughter, Becky. This spoke of a relationship between two people that would never be broken.

As a young child, Becky would be quite shy and retiring, and she chose who she communicated with carefully, and with great deliberation. You would think that this trait would be something a child would not be capable of, but don't be fooled; Becky knew exactly what she was doing even under the age of five. Like my son Chris, Becky would look you up and down then decide if she liked you or not. If she didn't like someone's energy, she would make it known to her Mum until they left and went home.

The instant I saw Becky. I fell in love, her eyes met mine, and the godmother and goddaughter bond were made. The bond between her mum, Helen, and me was also one of those bonds, friends since childhood, and forty years later, here we are an unbroken bond, and friends forever.

When Helen asked me to be Becky's godparent, I was so proud. I will never forget the christening day. It was quite funny when the Vicar read out the ceremony, I was one of the godparents standing waiting to read our pledge. Then the Vicar turned to us and said, "Now, Godparents, repeat after me." I was the only one of the godparents who repeated our part of the ceremony. The whole church lay silent as I repeated word for word God's expectations of a godparent. But of course, everyone was supposed to speak, but all you could hear was my quiet voice receiving my responsibilities as a new godmother. But at that moment although I felt embarrassed as I was the only one speaking, I thought that it was meant to be. From that day to this, Becky and I have had the most beautiful relationship, I love her dearly and always will.

My life was never easy at this time, as I had a child who was suffering from the worst form of social anxiety. But Chris always loved to be at Helen's house, it was one of his safe havens, so this meant I saw a lot of Becky, and I was a big part of her childhood memories.

It was probably around the age of two that we noticed that there were certain times and particular people Becky didn't want to be around. This would make her very anxious, and she would be desperate to leave. It was then we knew that she could see through people, into their souls. If they were not all they were pretending to be on the outside, then Becky knew it. People and the way they conducted themselves always bothered Becky, and she certainly didn't suffer fools lightly even at a young age.

Becky chose her friends carefully, and on starting school at the age of five, she began to make new friendships. It wasn't until she reached the age of twelve, and had to start senior school, that social anxieties began to hit her. It was caused by that transition from being a child to suddenly being thrust into the world of teenagers and having to grow up in one day! I know of many parents who would agree with me when I say that the day the Government closed the doors on what we called the middle school is when anxiety was heightened in our children. I feel that 90% of children need that transition; they need to be nurtured into the senior school not thrown to the lions. If the Government looked at this, then much-needed resources would be saved.

When Becky started with anxiety, her mum was at her wits' end. It was a bad time for me then, as Christopher's father had also just died, so I was going through Hell myself with Chris. Nothing Helen did seemed to help; advice comes from everywhere when your child starts with anxiety, the one that sticks with me is, "Just make them do it!" You cannot make someone who is suffering from anxiety do anything they don't want to do. It cripples them, and they are frozen in time. If they don't want to do something it isn't because they are challenging you, it is because they cannot breathe and their heart is beating at a hundred miles an hour, it is never because they are naughty.

Helen and her family moved from Wallasey to a rural area, and it was at that point, things went from bad to worse. We do these things because we think it will help, but moving schools isn't always a good idea when your child is suffering so.

The school Becky moved to is a school near Heswall. It was where things took a turn for the worst, and would you believe that it was those running the school that caused most of the problems? There was no support for children with any mental health issues, zero tolerance and zero support. I would go weekly to visit and stay for my tea, many times staying over with Becky and Helen as Helen's husband worked away at this time. Helen would light the fire, and we would have cosy pyjama evenings. Becky would always sit on the beanbag in front of me and ask me to give her some Reiki. I used to beg the Reiki masters to heal Becky.

We realised that Reiki helped Becky to sleep right through the night, as part of her anxiety was that she couldn't get to sleep. Reiki has a way of relaxing every part of you, including your mind. Helen has a friend called Kim, who is such a beautiful soul, she isn't Reiki trained, but she has this incredible ability of bringing in a calming and healing energy, so between the two of us, we would give this to Becky as often as we could. Healing can come in all shapes and sizes, and the one thing Kim and I had in common was that we both had loved Becky dearly, so this intention was always pure.

I have asked Becky to give me her side of this story, as with the other people in this book, I think this is important to hear how they felt on their own journey.

So, in Becky's words, here is the story of her journey.

Becky

My anxiety was horrible; it overwhelmed me at times, but lucky for me, it only really affected me within my school environment, which some people found hard to understand, me included! But as it was just within the walls of that place where my fear first started, I knew that this was a place I did not want to be. My anxiety made me feel withdrawn and different to my peers who didn't understand what I was going through, as I was fine when I was not in school. Even the thought of school made me anxious, the pressure of having to go was horrible, and my mum would get annoyed as she didn't understand what was happening either and she wasn't getting the support that she needed. The school just pressured her into sending me in, as the education system and the law said I had to go to school!

So, with this added stress on my mum, this heightened my own anxiety, and I used to spiral into a hellish place every morning. This was a place I never thought I would ever be free from. I received some support in school, from one of the teachers, who seemed to understand anxiety, but it really wasn't enough. With limited resources and limited patience, the school basically pushed anxiety aside. My mum paid for a counsellor, but that made me worse for some reason. On reflection, I know that the only way to cure what I was going through was to take me out of that situation. I think I lived with it for such a long time, but nobody could help me but me. I hated the way school made me anxious, and this alone really made me feel so incredibly low and depressed at times. Looking back now, it was quite barbaric how I, and others who were suffering from anxiety, were treated, and I felt the education system needed to be more supportive.

It was at this time the school had a new Head of Year. He did not know me but judged me, as being a naughty teenager who didn't want to be at school. He was quite an angry man and was only interested in his school statistics, and I was jeopardising them! How wrong he was. I was a good student who longed to be happy. I had a good relationship with all my friends and teachers and considering my anxiety heightened in a school environment, I managed to do very well. But towards my final year I just couldn't cope anymore, every night I would dread going to sleep knowing the next day I would have to go into school, knowing the horrible way the anxiety would affect me.

I would physically shake and my heartfelt as though it was going to burst! I couldn't breathe, it was so frightening. My mum was so supportive, but she was at a loss as to what to do next. She was tired of watching me suffer, so she decided that enough was enough! No more making me go through this every day of my life. So, for the next couple of weeks of school, before I finally got to leave, she told me that I was only going to go in for my exams and insisted that school sent work home. She held a meeting with the Headmaster, which was awful, as he had no understanding of my illness, he just became angrier. I wrote him a letter telling him how I felt, and this made things worse, he was now angrier than ever and told my mum how awful I was for writing such terrible things.

The letter I sent him was pleading for his help, but he said that it was rude and should not have been sent into him. My mum was confused because she had read the letter before she took it to the Headmaster. He told mum that I had used the word **mental health,** which was not acceptable! In which he quoted "I do not like that language from your daughter." Mum looking quite shocked, replied, "My daughter has not sworn and never has!" He then told mum that he was referring to the use of the word **mental health!** He did not like those words and felt anxiety did not come under that label and that I should not be labelling myself.

I had lived with it for five years by this time, so I knew exactly what I was dealing with, as my mum said he was blind and ignorant to my needs, and it was at this point she decided enough was enough! Although the staff in the unit tried to help me, they really did not understand the complexities of anxiety and panic attacks and were pushing me and others over the edge.

My mum had lost faith in school, and it was at this point, she decided to take the pressure off me and took things into her own hands. She took me out of school. This was a huge relief and I felt myself again!

During this horrible time, my Auntie Lynn would come and give me Reiki to help me sleep, which was such a relief as I didn't sleep very well at all. Reiki helped me to feel uplifted and helped to clear my head. It made me realise that I had to be brave and face this head on. A The only thing that could do that was to not be thrown into the environment that triggered it.

I had coped alone for so long, always keeping it to myself for fear of feeling different, but once I'd left the place that triggered the anxiety I did feel it was then I was finally free, and I haven't looked back since. I have managed to put it all behind me, but still, I find it hard to speak about this as it does bring all those emotions flooding back.

I now work with young children and feel my experiences have given me the patience and the understanding to help these kids. I can see the symptoms of anxiety within an instant of being around these bright young children, and I can sit with them and help them in a way that school never helped me. I love my job, and I hope that I am making a difference now out in this world that has been so uneducated about the devastating effects of anxiety within youngsters of today.

Helen (mum)

As a mum, it was very much the hardest time ever having to make your child do the things that triggered her anxiety. With no help from the system and being threatened with Court if my daughter did not attend, I regularly received attendance letters from school reminding me that my child's attendance was going against the school policy. This, of course, just made the situation worse. It was so hard because I could see my daughter falling apart, but they were only interested in their attendance figures. I believe the school now has taken on board the mental health problems that are within some of the children today, and now offer support for children and parents who are going through the same as we had. This was all too late for Becky; the ignorance of the school and the rudeness of the Headmaster just made our lives a living hell!

I suffered myself by making my child go to school. Many people, including doctors, told me that

172

this was the right thing to do. I was told by a counsellor that I wasn't to beat myself up over this as being forced by a Government system also put me under great stress. On reflection, I didn't agree, I didn't feel it helped I know it made everything much worse. It had a significant impact on her life at the time. She just needed someone to understand her and know just how frightening it was to be suffering and having a full-blown panic attack, and then being forced, physically at times, to go to school. When I reflect now, how can that possibly help anybody? It made me feel desperate, and I can sympathise with any parent who has physically had to force a terrified teenager, out of the door and to school because the education policies, the law and this country tells you that's what we must do.

I do feel it has made my daughter stronger, wiser, more caring, and capable, after living under the pressure of anxiety for so long. She has now come out on top and hopefully will never have to deal with this type of stress again. Becky loved to receive Reiki from Lynn, and I could see it helped her to sleep, and bring her a certain amount of calmness for that short time. I know now that Reiki and other holistic treatments have become a part of society, as the issue of anxiety has significantly increased.

I hope that children today are not having to battle as hard as Becky and I had to and are being understood instead of being pushed aside.

173

In Conclusion

On reading this book, I hope you have picked up the desperate need for the world to sit up and listen to these frantic people. Mental health is no joke! It is the invisible illness that attacks when you least expect it and affects people of all ages.

I have been led to believe that those who are suffering from any mental illness are tuned into their Spirit Guides and the Angels. Hundreds of years ago, many would have been put into lunatic asylums and had to undergo cruel treatments to bring them back from their state of mind. But of course, this didn't work; it just convinced these poor people that the world was cruel.

People like me would have been locked up that's for sure! Every time I said I had a voice in my head giving me information, it would have brought me closer to electric shock treatments!! This was barbaric and cruel, and just because you cannot see something doesn't mean it isn't there.

I am writing this concluding chapter on 27/12/2019 just four days before the most influential year of the century hits us all. 2020 is a year of understanding, and everyone will be lifted out of the Neanderthal way of thinking and into the real world. It is time to take off those blinkers and admit that there is something else out there.

Benjamin Franklin proved that lightening was full of electricity and experimented with it until he realised it could be harnessed to make light. He believed that he could make it work, and it would make a massive difference to millions of people across the world. Was he laughed at? Yes! Could you see this thing he believed was there for all to harness? No, not until that energy was harnessed and it lit up the world, then everyone believed in his theory.

Alexandra Graham Bell told the world that he could transmit voices which would be heard through a line called a telephone. People will have laughed and called him crazy, but on March 10th, 1876, he made the very first phone call ever, and the world went mad! Everyone wanted a telephone.

People will have mocked both men and told them that they were crazy, just like we spiritual mediums have been mocked in the past.

But I will leave you with this thought. I hear voices in my head. I receive messages from teachers who cannot be seen with the naked eye and who live in another dimension. Does this mean we are mad? Or does it imply we have tapped into a high energy source which has been at our disposal for eternity?

The children of today will no longer be forgotten. They will be heard, and because their energy is far superior to anyone else's they will lead this world differently, without greed or a desperate need for money. What they do will be because they want to spread the word of love and peace.

They will encourage others to be the best possible version of themselves, inspiring achievements, and not showing jealousy of their neighbours or friends. They will encourage everyone to work within the light, and that, my friend, will be a different world to the one in which we live in now.

I am extremely excited about the future of Lynn Robinson Spiritual Hub. I reopened the doors, to my spiritual retreats with great success in 2019. The reviews have been remarkable, and people rebook with 99% of the time.

The retreats have been designed with you in mind. To bring calm and some much-needed headspace to all who attend. We serve home-cooked food and baking, to feed your body, meditation, and Karuna Reiki to feed your soul.

I offer guidance and a listening ear to all who want to spend time with us at our stunning locations.

Check out my website for more details on up and coming events and retreats. I am taking bookings for the end of the summer, 2020 once it is safe for us all to venture out into the world again.

I believe many are suffering since the lockdown, with all sorts of mental health, and I do think that a weekend with us will bring you calm and peace.

I wish you all love and light. May the light find its way into your soul, because once it does, you will no longer want to be anywhere else. Spirituality is not a job; it is within us from birth, it is beautiful, but it is never a comfortable journey. People will fall away from you, but this is because your light is too bright for them.

During hard times when you cannot find the sunshine, be the sunshine, and bring that love and light to others.

ABOUT THE AUTHOR

Lynn Robinson was born in the 1960s in Wirral,
England and grew up like many others in a working-
class family.
She has overcome many obstacles in her life to bring
her to where she is today.
Lynn is a loving wife, mother of three and has one
stepson; she has three beautiful granddaughters
and two grandsons.
During the years leading up to writing her first book,
she worked in the corporate world. She was quite the
entrepreneur, but it soon became apparent that this
was not her pathway forward. Since a young age,
Lynn would communicate and see the angels around
her.
Lynn set out to discover what these messages meant
and how to become closer to the divine spirit and
work with the angels. She was guided by the spirit
world for many years and told she would write a book
but had no idea when.
She now teaches private classes every week of
likeminded people, who want to understand what
their messages and feelings they are experiencing are
about.
In 2016 Lynn sat down and wrote the first of many
chapters to her book 'A Light to Guide us Home'.
This book sets out Lynn's life story and how her
Spirit Guides and her Guardian Angel brought her to
where she is today.

When published this book made number 1 best seller on Amazon.

The sequel to her first book is Angels Around us, messages from heaven. This book was published in January 2019 and was a great success and made number 1 best seller on Amazon.

Lynn sat down early 2019 to write this book The Forgotten Lynn has seen first-hand the suffering that mental health causes individuals and families and she wanted to share some of her experiences with others to help them to realise that they are not alone.

Her mission is to help as many people as she can to find the light within themselves and to help them realise that they are not alone, and they are guided daily.

---

www.lynn-robinson-spiritual-hub.co.uk
F: @mediumlynnrobinson
Insta: lynnrobinson_
Twitter: @LROBINSONMEDIUM

Printed in Great Britain
by Amazon